RHINEBECK'S HISTORIC
Beekman Arms

BRIAN PLUMB & MATTHEW PLUMB

Charleston London

THE
History
PRESS

Published by The History Press
Charleston, SC 29403
www.historypress.net

Front cover, top: 1873 fire pumper. *Courtesy Museum of Rhinebeck History*; *bottom*: 2013 photo by author.
Back cover, top: circa 1915 car. *Courtesy Rhinebeck Historical Society*; *bottom*: Postcard and envelope.
Courtesy of the Beekman Arms; 1800 background map. *Courtesy Library of Congress*.

First published 2014

Manufactured in the United States

ISBN 978.1.62619.036.8

Library of Congress CIP data applied for.

Notice: The information in this book is true and complete to the best of our knowledge. It is offered without guarantee on the part of the author or The History Press. The author and The History Press disclaim all liability in connection with the use of this book.

Contents

Undated, but after the circa 1873 town hall was built. The picture shows the new lawn, planted trees and a replacement pump put in by Griffin Hoffman. This may possibly be the very first photo showing the third-floor addition. *A rare photo courtesy of Terence Boylan.*

Preface

One day; and now with hunger, thirst, fatigue,
Almost o'ercome, with most rejoicing eyes
A tavern sign he at the distance spies:
Approaching on the sign these words appear:
"For man & beast best entertainment here."

—A History of Travel in America, *Seymour Dunbar*[1]

In days of old, long before commercial stagecoaches (1785), steamboats (1807), trains (1850) and the widespread use of automobiles (1908), man traveled any significant distance solely by sailing ship or horseback. The continent's rivers and connected lakes were the primary means of inland access, but winter ice, along with the desire to go in directions inaccessible by water, made the forest paths just as important. Centuries-old Native American trails, such as the Westchester Path, the Minisink Trail, the Wickquasgeck Trail and a multitude of unnamed Lenape and Mahican trails up the Hudson River were some of the first pathways followed by the early European explorers. Along their routes, the country's first non-coastal towns would be settled.

Inland travel in these early days was both arduous and filled with some amount of danger. Horse and man could only travel twenty to twenty-five miles before requiring physical rest and nourishment. Darkness and weather often limited mobility. Muddy and unmarked trails, river crossings and the presence of any rogues, wild animals or natives in the area added to the difficulties. For the weary traveler, any safe stop through the wilderness must have been a welcome sight.

It was the pioneering early settlers who often opened their homes to these infrequent travelers, thus becoming the first "wayside taverns" of their day. As the population grew and travel increased, these rural homes became businesses, establishing the first true taverns, public houses, ordinaries and inns of colonial America. Offering "entertainment" (food and shelter) for both man and his beast, they soon came to serve as the centers for all communication, trade, governance and protection.

By the early 1700s, several of the native paths in colonial New York had grown into officially designated travel routes. The two most important were the main "Post Roads"—one to the east connecting the seaport of New York City to the British colonies in New England (the Boston Post Road), and the other to the north, the Albany Post Road, connecting New York to the Old Dutch trading center renamed Albany.

Paralleling the east bank of the Hudson River, the early Albany Post Road passed through the wilderness before reaching the more established colonial settlements in the areas of Philipsburg, Peekskill, Fishkill, Poughkeepsie, Rhinebeck, Claverack and Kinderhook. Remarkably, while much of the Post Road has long been paved over and incorporated into Route 9, there still exist vestiges of the old historic dirt road. In Putnam County across from West Point, a stretch of the original road, known as the Old Albany Post Road, skirts the eastern side of the lower Hudson Highlands. For these 6.6 miles, residents have fought hard to retain the original rugged setting, milestone markers and all. Driving up it, even in a modern automobile, you can get a good sense of what the old Post Road was like. On the northern terminus, the road reaches an old circa 1761 stage stop once known as Warren's Tavern.[2] The tavern appears out of nowhere after a long, isolated, hilly trek—seemingly a welcome respite for horsemen and stage riders. The road was much like this, though considerably less improved, all the way to the "Ferry at Crawlier over against the City of Albany."[3] There were but few settlements in between and few other trails.

In the area that later became Rhinebeck, a notable trail intersection did occur. On the opposite side of the Hudson River, an ancient pathway existed that followed the Esopus and Rondout Creeks all the way to the Delaware River. The "path" extended east directly across the Hudson to the Rhinebeck shore. From here, it picked up a footpath referred to as the Sepasco Trail.[4] Near the intersection of this footpath and the original Post Road, forged two miles east of the river on the upper plateau called "the flatts," stood a freshwater spring and another of these isolated homes, one of first few on the entire road. This was the house of William Traphagen, Rhinebeck's first settler, built on lands obtained from the original patentee, Henry Beekman. Like all remote homes along travel routes, it, too, must have served as an early tavern, fort, assembly hall and trading post.

William was busy creating a new world here in this isolated wilderness. On this land, he was raising and protecting his family of five, clearing forest, splitting rail fences to keep the bears and wolves out, tilling his soil, caring for livestock, applying his trade, constructing the mill and church, minding to travelers, befriending natives, attending to civic duties and simply trying to survive and bring some prosperity to his young family. All this in twenty-two years, from roughly 1716 to 1738 (remarkably, starting when he was age fifty-two). His daughter Geesje would take over his house or build one close by. His sons William Jr. and Arent would also have homes and farms here. A generation later, Geesje's son Simon, a merchant, appears to be responsible for building the structure at the crossroads that would become the Beekman Arms.

By 1802, and now on its third owner, Simon's old dwelling was clearly operating as a prominent hotel. Since that time, it has continued on virtually uninterrupted (a few renovations and seasonal closings aside), providing "entertainment" to all its guests. Famous and ordinary wayfarers for seven generations and counting would cross over its threshold. Though other taverns were made more famous by being singled out in verse (Longfellow's Wayside Inn) or momentary historic occasion (Washington's farewell address at Fraunces' Tavern, or the use of Concord MA's Wright Tavern by British Major Pitcairn one fateful day in 1775), few were as central to a town as the Beekman Arms was and likely will always continue to be. It is a workhorse as well as an icon.

RESEARCHING RHINEBECK'S PAST

Anyone conducting research on Rhinebeck immediately stumbles on two old books: *History of Rhinebeck* by Edward M. Smith, published in 1881, and *Historic Old Rhinebeck, Echoes of Two Centuries,* by Howard H. Morse, published twenty-seven years later in 1908. This was the post-Romantic era, often called "the Age of Realism." The Civil War and the country's centennial in 1876 had rekindled this generation's patriotic spirit, sense of duty and reverence for the past. At the same time, advances since the Industrial Revolution were by now exponentially accelerating change. In a way, the country was moving forward so quickly that the past was being left behind. This was not lost on some. A few historians thankfully took to the pen, recording the old stories and "facts" from the village elders before both slipped away. These rich, verisimilarly written histories can be found for many cities and towns. In many cases, they are all that exist.

While Mr. Smith's book was more of a biographical study, Mr. Morse, a prominent attorney and Civil War veteran who grew up in Rhinebeck, endeavored for over forty-two years to write a more comprehensive story. Both are to be respected for their efforts, as they have left us useful and well-written histories.

As researchers following in their footsteps over one hundred years later, it is easy to get pulled into these versions of history and then quote them as fact. It seems just about everyone has. The authors did live closer in time to when the history was being made, so sources were fresher, and presumably less history was lost by then. Unfortunately, neither work is annotated or footnoted. Though source references are sometimes given, often we are just left to take the authors' word for it. Also, somewhat surprisingly, they provide very little, and to a degree contradictory, information on Traphagen and the tavern's early history. Morse starts the formal "Traphagen Tavern" lore seemingly all on his own (he claims William built the first tavern, it was too small, so Arent built the next one [the Beekman Arms]). Smith never even mentions the Traphagens building a tavern; they simply owned the land the Beekman Arms was built on. Other early histories seem to follow this pattern. In addition to the two Rhinebeck books, three histories of Dutchess County were written. The authors, Philip Smith (1877), James Smith (1882) and Frank Hasbrouck (1909), all fail to provide any additional insight. In their tales of Rhinebeck, the 1877 history neglects entirely to even mention Traphagen and the tavern (though Traphagen should have been noted as one of the first settlers in the county), and unsurprisingly, the 1882 history follows Smith's 1881 published history, and the 1909 history follows Morse's 1908 history. Morse and Smith likely can be relied on for their contemporary knowledge, and we do so on occasion in this book. We also use them, guardedly, when no other "color" is available to help tell the story.

While it is surprising that the early history of such a (now) notable structure had not been formally recorded, there are a few possible reasons for this lapse. How the building was actually being used at the time (dwelling or business), the economic climate of the day, commerce routes (i.e., the Hudson River was a more important north–south freight route than the Post Road), competition and the landlord's status in the community all undoubtedly impacted its importance. Owners were probably more concerned with just trying to keep their businesses going than thinking about—much less recording—the history being made there. Not being descendant-owned, there was also less concern about ancestors and legacy. Newspapers usually help tell the story, but being some distance from any large city where papers existed, Rhinebeck and the Beekman Arms (the BA) went virtually unnoticed. The local paper, the *Rhinebeck Gazette* (RG), is only archived, spottily, back to 1846.[5]

Local history books also seem to be filled with the more colorful stories of the connected Beekman and Livingston families, as well as the early circa 1686 settlement in Kipsbergen (renamed Rhinecliff in 1849). Volumes are written on these. Pink's Corner, where today's Routes 9 and 9G intersect, was another developing competing town center with its own tavern (Moul's). Up on the flatts where the Post Road came through, the old structure at the crossroad just seemed to be taken for granted.

Notably though, when the structure now known as the Beekman Arms is found mentioned in historical references, it always seems to be held in higher esteem, serving as a dignified "hotel" over that of roustabout colonial tavern. It was the place to bring visiting dignitaries and to celebrate any occasion. Its front lawn was the gathering place for every important event in town. Its location and substantial presence naturally drew in the business, political and traveling crowd. Just about all travel to the river passed by its doorstep, and we find former landlords were even engaged in the merchant and transport businesses. At the turn of the nineteenth century, we do know the business did exist, and at the turn of the twentieth century, we already see the building being celebrated as a treasured landmark.

Uncovering and documenting the actual history and giving the BA its rightful dues we felt was an important contribution to the town's historical record. We dug through state and local archives, county deeds and mortgages, tax and census data, wills (kept by the courts since 1752), town records, dozens of old maps and books, published newspaper articles, private collections of rare old photographs and preserved firsthand stories, historical society collections, church archives and larger archival collections, such as the Edward Livingston Papers in Princeton University, the New York Historical Society Morgan Lewis Papers and the New York State Archives (NYSA) in Albany. In addition, we conducted interviews with past owners, employees and local experts, and we looked for physical clues from the attic to the basement.

The trail was often hard to follow through the foggy dew of time. It is no wonder both Smith and Morse did not have clear facts to present—this story is simply not very transparent. Old deeds contained mistakes and reference points no longer valid, misinformation was abundant and official records were found missing, to name a few challenges. Innkeeper licenses, for example, were required per statutes dating to 1665 (and taverns in Dutchess County were regulated by 1763).[6] These records do not exist in one large, managed, state or county archive; they have always been kept locally. The earliest innkeeping license for the Beekman Arms still on record only dates to 1863.[7]

For some historical claims, we are left with just hearsay and undocumented fanciful legends. The more outrageous ones can be removed from the story with supporting evidence to the contrary (such as Washington sitting in the window watching travelers go by), but one cannot rule out every story entirely. The lack of proof does not necessarily mean some did not happen. The analytical process does force us to question past assertions, but in the end, hopefully readers will see this book as an "updating" of the history using today's technology and one hundred years of further data collection, not a disparaging of past notable work.

A book like this would not have been possible without the help of others. We are grateful for the assistance and knowledge of Michael Frazier from the Rhinebeck Historical Society (RHS). It would have been difficult to write this book without his help and generosity. Many thanks also to town historian Nancy Kelly, Beverly Kane from the Museum of Rhinebeck History (MRH), Ray Armater of Historic Hudson Valley (HHV) and David Byars of Hudson River Heritage (HRH) who all helped immeasurably. Special thanks to George and Phebe Banta, owners of the Beekman Arms, as well as former owner Charles LaForge, for supporting and encouraging this effort from the beginning and also for all their contributions. Thanks to Rick Winne for allowing us to review his grandfather's scrapbooks. Thanks to Chris Brooks of Kansas City, a noted Traphagen/Ostrander family authority, who helped us explore the early family history. Thanks to Dutchess County historian William Tatum for tracking down many of the ancient documents we needed and to local history legends Kay Verilli, John Winthrop Aldrich and Cynthia Owen Philip for their early input. Thanks to James Nannery, Johanna VanderVeer Bruno and Thomas Arata for their research assistance; to Terence Boylan for his photo and research help; to Peggy LaBelle for gaining access to the Dows tapes; and to the Dutchess County Geographic Information Services office and Vincent Arata for their mapping advice. We also want to thank the staffs at the Beekman Arms, Dutchess County Historical Society, Dutchess County and Ulster County Registry of Deeds (DCRD), Dutchess County Surrogate Court, Reformed Dutch Church of Rhinebeck, Kingston Historical Society, Red Hook Historical Society, Clermont State Historic Site, Franklin D. Roosevelt Presidential Library, Princeton University Library/Archives, Syracuse University Archives, New York State Archives (NYSA), New York State Public Library, New York Public Library, New York Historical Society, Albany Hall of Records, Adriance Library and the American Antiquarian Society (AAS), which all helped along the way. Thanks to Whitney Landis, our editor at The History Press, who championed this project and was of great help getting it to the finish line. Finally, thanks sincerely to Catherine Plumb, Mike Frazier, Joe Barbieri, Nancy Kelly and Beverly Kane for their review and comments on the manuscript.

Introduction

Een weinig bewaard is beter dan alles verloren.
A little preserved is better than all lost.
—*Old Dutch saying*

Ten years before the Pilgrims stepped ashore in Plymouth, the Dutch had already arrived in the Hudson Valley.[8] Henry Hudson's exploration in 1609 led to seasonal trading posts in 1610 and to the early settlements of Fort Nassau (1614), Fort Orange (1624) and New Amsterdam (1625). The Dutch would gain footholds down the coast and across lower New York all the way to the Delaware River. Beverwijck, near Forts Orange and Nassau, was established in 1652 by the growing population of fur traders settling in the area. The English forcefully took control of the region in 1664 and renamed Beverwijck "Albany" and New Amsterdam "New York." Esopus, later called Wiltwijck, the third-largest settlement (founded in 1653), was renamed "Kingston." The Dutch briefly regained control in 1673–74 but finally ceded the entire colony to England in the negotiated peace of the Third Anglo-Dutch War. In exchange, the Dutch received claim to Suriname and the East Indies spice island Pulau Run.

It was important to the English that the area be settled, as this helped lay their claim to the land and keep it out of the hands of the next territorial raider, France. It also pushed the natives aside. Conflict came, first with harassing raids and then with more organized attacks. The First and Second Esopus Wars came in 1659 and 1663.[9] In 1675, King Phillip (a native chief)

Watercolor sketch of the "Proposed Coat of Arms for New Amsterdam, New Netherland: Preparatory Drawing for a Presentation to the Dutch West India Company," circa 1630. *Courtesy of the New York Historical Society.*

began his war in the New England colonies. In 1688, King William's War had begun in the northern territories, including the Champlain Valley. In 1690, the French and Indians staged an infamous raid known as the "Schenectady Massacre" against the Dutch and English settlers just northwest of Albany, killing sixty people, including ten women and twelve children. In 1745, French and Indian forces raided Saratoga during King George's War, killing thirty. Raids and attacks continued even after the French and Indian War (1754–63) had been fought. The English endured. For them, integral ties to the land and to the people brought order, loyalty, commerce, tax revenue, natural resources, intelligence and a fighting force when called on. To stimulate settlement, the queen and later king of England, as well as their royal extended family and designated governors, began issuing "manors," "patents" and other forms of land grants to individuals who had the capacity to carry out the wishes of the monarchy.[10]

Wealthy and politically influential families were obtaining these grants and amassing great estates during this period, pushing in all directions from the earlier settlements. In 1697 and, more definitively, in 1703, Judge Henry Beekman of Kingston, son of William Beekman (a prosperous merchant and friend of the last Dutch Director-General, Pieter Stuyvesant), obtained two patents for land across the river in Dutchess County. One of these patents was for the greater Rhinebeck area. Land was wealth, and to begin monetizing some of this and fulfilling the terms of the patent issuance (principally Beekman's payment of forty schillings a year to the crown for this patent), Beekman began selling and leasing acreage, negotiating rents, finding settlers (such as the Palatines, who came in 1715) and building mills and docks.[11] When a colonial law in 1703 set forth the requirement to establish a Post Road to Albany, Morse tells us Beekman made sure the route ran through his land holding.

Beekman's first recorded sale was to Kingston resident William Traphagen on May 25, 1705. Beekman sold him a considerable stake, 281 acres, bounded by the Landsman Kill and Rhinebeck Kill to the west, south and north and by a line later defined as running on the east approximately at the angle of Oak Street (originally "Beginneth at a furr tree marked wth three notches & a Cross by a fall in ye first abovementioned run of water on Lantsmans Kill thence Running north north west fourty five minutes northerly along ye Lands of Coll Beekman to a White Oak tree marked as above fifty five chains").[12] This eastern boundary was resurveyed and redefined over time, as this initial measurement proved to be unacceptable. Old surveys and maps were notoriously imprecise, leading to frequent misunderstandings and disputes. The imprecision and inaccuracies were partly due to the equipment, science and recording methods of the day, but the real difficulty came in actually taking the measurements. Though sparsely settled by natives and cleared in places, this area was predominantly old-growth forest. Accurately stretching sixty-six-foot surveying chains through this terrain and getting proper line-of-sight compass readings had to be a formidable task.

Traphagen was to pay six schillings annually for this property. One of Beekman's account books, preserved in the Princeton University archives, records his tallying of payments from William. In 1706, Traphagen sold twenty-four acres of this land to Jacob Kip. This is notable because Traphagen was still listed as a resident of Kingston on the deed; he likely did not settle across the river yet. In "1710/11," Beekman sold more land to Traphagen, still of Kingston. In 1717, William's name starts appearing on Dutchess County tax and census records. In 1719, William sold six acres back to Beekman's son so he could build mills on the Landsman Kill, here on the flatts. Morse suggests that Beekman brought Traphagen to this land to help

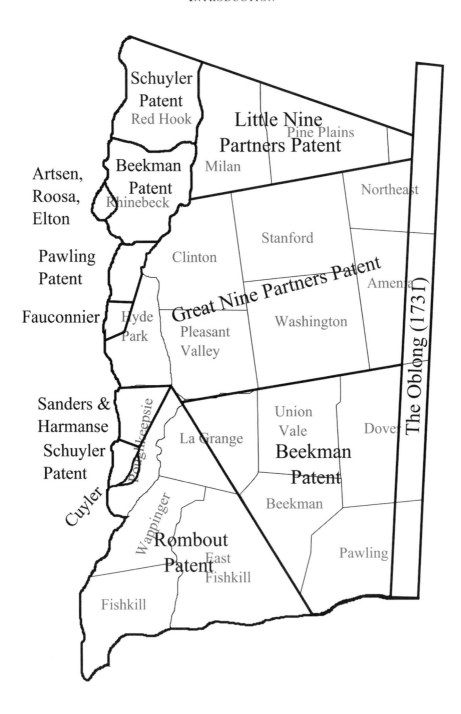

Schuyler
Patent
Red Hook

Little Nine
Partners Patent

Pine Plains

Artsen,
Roosa,
Elton

Beekman
Patent

Milan

Rhinebeck

Northeast

Pawling
Patent

Stanford

Clinton

Fauconnier

Great Nine Partners Patent

Amenia

Hyde
Park

Pleasant
Valley

Washington

The Oblong (1731)

Sanders &
Harmanse

Union
Vale

Dover

La Grange

Schuyler
Patent

Beekman
Patent

Cuyler

Beekman

Rombout
Patent

Wappinger

East
Fishkill

Pawling

Fishkill

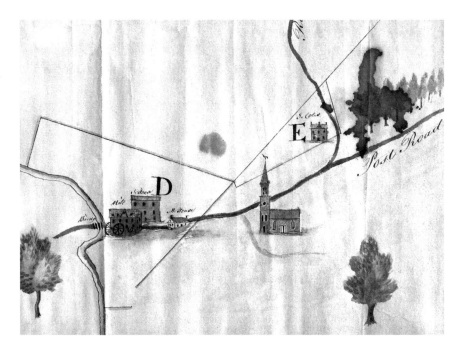

Above: Excerpt from "Map of a parcel of Land Conveyed by Coll. Henry Beekman Dec. to William Traphagen." This map contains a date reference to November 24, 1769. The two-story structure labeled S. Coles is the Beekman Arms. The road branching to the top is West Market Street heading toward the river. The circa 1731 Dutch Reformed Church shown would be rebuilt in its present form in 1807–08. Nothing remains of the once substantial Beekman mill. *Courtesy of the Princeton University Library.*

Opposite: Dutchess County, highlighting Beekman's two patents. The larger one to the south covered the towns of Beekman, Union Vale, Dover, Pawling and part of LaGrange. Dutchess County was established in 1683, but given that it was so sparsely populated, it was administered by Ulster County (in Kingston) until 1713. To the north, the area around Livingston Manor (Germantown, Clermont) was carved out in 1799 and given to Columbia County. Dutchess County also originally included all of Putnam County to the south before 1812.

build the first mill. This is unfounded but entirely plausible, as Traphagen appears to be a craftsman. On the 1705 and 1706 deeds, he specifically titles himself as a "wheelwright." Traphagen's late age, essential skills and the size and location of the property he was able to negotiate (perhaps his compensation) would seem to support this assertion.[13]

In 1746, there was a notable land exchange between Judge Henry Beekman's son, Henry Jr., and William's son, Arent Traphagen. This exchange gave Beekman two and a third more acres around his six-acre mill property on the Landsman Kill in town, and Arent received a one-and-a-half-acre triangular lot that seemed to adjoin his house. By 1769, there is evidence this triangular lot contained the two-story structure that would later become the Beekman Arms.

THE BEEKMAN ARMS

The first ever illustration and mention of the building itself is on the 1769 Princeton map. "S. Coles" is found above the structure, but it is not clear if it is a business or simply a residence. "S. Coles" is Simon Isaac Cole, William Traphagen's grandson, and he identifies himself on old deeds as a "merchant" (cited by Morse as the first merchant in town). Rhinebeck maps in 1796 and 1798 simply show the building as belonging to another

The original Beekman Arms sign hung outside, April 1918. The Beekman coat-of-arms gave the inn its name. The owners in that era generously gave the date as 1700, which obviously could not be true. The area was not even settled until 1715. The building called "White Corner" is behind the sign. Built before 1858, it was razed in 1940 for an Esso gas station. White Corner was used for many purposes over the years and held a store, post office and bank. Morse states, "The store became the business forum...a leading factor in town, village, and county affairs." To the left of it are a plumbing store, a grocer and a barbershop. Farther over is a restaurant/saloon. *Courtesy of Historic Hudson Valley, the Dows Collection.*

BEEKMAN ARMS
OLDEST HOTEL IN AMERICA
W. W. FOSTER, PROP'R.
OPEN ALL THE YEAR

1700   1917

RHINEBECK, NEW YORK
DUTCHESS COUNTY

Very first postcard after the renovation, dated 1917. Starting from at least 1907, the Beekman Arms claimed to be the "Oldest Hotel in America." It started changing to oldest "inn" during the mid- to late 1970s.

merchant named Bogardus with no inn or tavern attribution. A few years later, an 1802 map labels it for the first time as a business—the word "Hotel" prominently appears next to the building. Morse gives the early BA the colorful names of Traphagen's Tavern, Bogardus' Tavern and Potter's Tavern, but none of these can be substantiated. On two separate 1810 maps, the BA is called "Jacques Hotel" and "Jaques Stagehouse," a name it famously carried for some thirty-two years. An 1834 deed also mentions "the Tavern House...commonly known as Jaques Place."[14] By 1858, it is labeled on a map as "M. Marquardt Hotel." An 1862 *Rhinebeck Gazette* ad notes it as "McElroy's Hotel." For most of its early life, however, it simply was called the Rhinebeck Hotel (1867, 1876 maps, photos, old ads) and colloquially referred to as the "Old Hotel." (Note that we will call it the "BA" through all the time periods for writing efficiency, trusting the reader will understand its application.)

It wasn't until 1917, when Wallace W. Foster, owner since 1914, took out a large mortgage and renovated the hotel that the name "Beekman Arms" came to be. The funding was used for extensive changes and modifications, and when done, it transformed the old grey stone hotel into the grand

Beekman Arms Landlords and Owners

Landlord (or manager)	From	To	Yrs	Owner	
Lot	1746	1747	0.5	Arent Traphagen	
1 House/Store	1766	1770	4	Simon I. Cole (nephew, heir of Arent Traphagen)	1
2 House/Store	1770	1799	30	Everardus Bogardus to 1799 to courts from 1799-1802	2
3 Asa Potter	1802	1805	4	Asa Potter	3
4 William Jacques	1805	1835	30	Elisha R. Potter until 1834, Richard Schell until 1837	4
5 Mrs. Jacques	1835	1837	2	Richard Schell	5
6 Jacob H. Tremper	1837	1840	3	Johnathan Wilson, probated until 1839, then Elisha Potter Jr	6
7 Robert T. Seymour	1840	1853	14	Elisha Potter Jr until 1845, then Van Keuren/Platt/Delamater	7
8 O.V. Doty	1853	1855	2	Garret Van Keuren, William Platt, Henry Delamater	8
9 David F. Sipperly	1855	1857	2	Van Keuren/others until 1856, Martin Marquart	
10 Edward Pultz	1857	1858	1	Martin Marquart	9
11 Hunting Germond	1858	1860	2	Marquart until 1859, Hunter Germond	10
12 Burnett Conklin	1860	1862	2	Hunter Germond until 1861, then James McElroy	11
13 Jas. N. McElroy	1862	1864	2	James McElroy	
14 Griffin Hoffman	1864	1873	9	Griffin Hoffman	12
15 Tremper Brothers	1873	1884	11	Tremper until foreclosed 1884, the Griffin Hoffman	13
16 Lorenzo Decker	1884	1891	7	heirs of Hoffman until 1889 then Catherine Fulmer, NH, RH	14
17 Edward Lasher	1891	1893	2	Catherine Fulmer, Nicholas Hoffman, Robert Hoffman	15
18 E.M. Vanderburgh	1893	1894	1	Catherine Fulmer, NH, RH	
19 Vernon D. Lake	1894	1906	12	Catherine Fulmer (alone) until 1904	
20 Halleck Welles	1906	1907	1	Halleck Welles	16
21 Arthur Shuffle	1907	1914	7	Arthur Shuffle	17
22 Wallace W. Foster	1914	1925	11	Wallace Foster	18
23 Tracy Dows, acting	1926	1927	1	Tied up in courts. Ownership claim by bank.	
24 Frank Lord, RM	1927	1929	3	Beekman Arms, Inc. (Tracy Dows)	19
25 Frank Cole, RM	1930	1930	1	Beekman Arms, Inc. (Tracy Dows)	
26 Lewis F. Winne	1930	1949	18	BA Inc. until 1939, Then 8 person local group (Winne, et.al.)	
27 Harry Williams	1949	1950	1	8 Person local group (new Beekman Arms, Inc.)	
28 Kenneth Arnold	1950	1952	2	8 Person local group (Beekman Arms, Inc.)	20
29 Howard Hohl	1952	1954	2	8 person local group (Beekman Arms, Inc.)	
30 Walter Harter	1954	1958	4	8 person local group (Beekman Arms, Inc.)	
31 Charles LaForge, Jr.	1958	2002	44	8 per. group until 1969, then Charles LaForge (WIONY Inc.)	21
32 George & Phebe Banta	2002	Present	12	George & Phebe Banta (Beekman Delamater Prop, LLC)	22
Possible Operation as a Store/Tavern/Hotel	1766	2014	248	*1766 date uncertain. Building existed by 1769.*	
Known Operation as a Hotel/Inn	1802	2014	**212**	*These dates are certain - in continuous opertion.*	

Ownership information obtained from a review of all the Dutchess and Ulster County deed and mortgage records related to this property. Early landlord information is from Morse and Smith and modified as required for accuracy. The first Beekman Arms, Inc., was principally owned by Tracy Dows. From 1927–29, he hired the Campbell Management Group to manage the hotel. Resident managers were employed.

whitewashed building it is today. With the new look came the rechristening to the "Beekman Arms." It is not recorded why the name was changed.[15] Ostensibly, with the renovations, Mr. Foster, later the proprietor of Foster's Coach House just up the road, or Tracy Dows, his financier (who later came to own the BA), wanted a fresh start with a more prestigious and commercially appealing name.

"Arms" is an abbreviation for "coat of arms," and it is not an armory reference. The Beekman crest had always hung outside the building on a signpost since the renovation. In ye old days when signboards were colorful and distinctive, the images were used to identify a particular business, such as the Queen's Head, Red Lion or, in this case, the Beekman [coat-of-] Arms. Going to the Beekman Arms is like saying going to the tavern with the Beekman coat-of-arms hung outside.[16]

The Beekman Arms' past includes a brick-a-brac of landlords and owners through the years, some holding it for at least ten years, others leaving after just one year of trying to make a go of it. Records indicate there have been thirty-two landlords and twenty-two owners to date. (The bronze plaque near the BA's entrance, put up by Charles LaForge, landlord/owner from 1958 to 2002, lists "landlords," which were not necessarily the owners.)

The landlords' stories, some lost through time, are all influenced heavily by the circumstances of their era. World wars, recessions, bank failures, technological improvements, politics, medical advances, epidemics, the arts and individual prosperity and mobility all impacted their tenures as hosts. Through all this, the old hotel ebbed and flowed in its own prosperity. There were several foreclosures, and there were at least six advertised renovations. How the Beekman Arms adapted and changed through all this is more than simply a story of how it looked and who owned it. Within and surrounding these changes is the story of the evolving community and growing nation.

TAVERNS, INNS AND HOTELS

We have so far used these terms interchangeably when referring to the BA. Until 1802 when we see it first labeled as a hotel, it is not clear what the BA was considered, if it was a business at all. Generally speaking, in the colonial period, as stipulated in the 1763 New York "Act to appoint Commissioners for licensing Taverns and reducing their Number in Dutchess County," there was no distinction between being called an inn or tavern; both terms were used, and they were considered to be synonymous.[17] In England, the tavern was generally a place where wine, ale, beer, other spirits, and perhaps food were served; the inn was a place that provided overnight lodging in addition to these refreshments. In colonial America, that distinction did not exist. The owner/landlord was entirely free to choose between the two. Regional influences played a part, as "inn" was seen more in Pennsylvania and "tavern" more in New York and New England.[18] To operate one, a 1773 act "for the better Regulation of the Public Inns and Taverns" covering Dutchess County spelled out that the innkeeper must "keep three good spare Beds, two of which to be Feather Beds, with good and sufficient sheeting and Covering for such Beds, respectively, and good and sufficient Stabling and Provender of Hay in the Winter, and Hay or Pasturage in the Summer, and Grain for six horses or other Cattle, for the accommodation of Travelers."[19]

"Ordinary," "public house" (later pub), "coffee house," "alehouse" and "tippling house" were other names for early colonial drinking and eating establishments. An ordinary in Britain served a prepared meal to the public at a set time for an established price. It was a commonly used term in early New England. "Boardinghouse" is also seen as a lodging reference, though typically for longer stays at lower prices. There once was one right across Mill Street from the Beekman Arms.

The term "hotel," of French origin, started appearing later, rising in use and prominence with the railroads. Hotels generally offered, or were thought to offer, "modern conveniences" (possibly clean sheets, separate beds, maid service, finer dining, etc.), and their primary business was lodging of guests. The first use of the word in the United States was in New York City, when Joseph Corre named his new Broadway establishment "Corre's Hotel" in 1790. The "City Hotel" near Trinity Church appeared in 1794, eventually becoming an important stage travel center.[20] Typically, they also had separate livery stables to care for the animals (up the street, not in the backyard, and perhaps owned by someone else). Once hotels became known for modern, more hygienic services (such as indoor plumbing, first seen at the Tremont Hotel in Boston in 1829), the term "tavern," connoting harder times and the old ways, seems to have become less attractive to use.

ALONG THE POST ROAD AND TO THE BEEKMANS

Before the hotel came the Post Road, but even before the road came the Beekmans. To better understand the BA's history, it is important to take a brief look at how the namesake Beekmans fit into the story.

The earliest innkeeping license on record for the BA, June 2, 1863. The earliest on file in the Rhinebeck records for any tavern is 1852 (to H.J. Knowles). Licenses were given to individuals, not to the building or business. *Courtesy of the Town of Rhinebeck.*

CHAPTER 1

The Early Beekmans

Rhinebeck's history is, in part, an intertwined genealogical record of some of the most influential early families in New York. The Livingstons, Beekmans, Schuylers, Pawlings, Rutsens, Kips and others all played a part, and their lives and landholdings are well documented. A brief refresher on the first four generations of the Beekmans will help explain the early BA story.[21]

WILHELMUS "WILLIAM" BEEKMAN (1623–1707), the forefather, came to New Amsterdam aboard the ship *Princess* in May 1647 with Director-General Pieter Stuyvesant. William was said to be an officer and/or clerk in the Dutch West India Company. He became a large landholder and served in several official capacities. In 1658, he was appointed governor of Christina, the former Swedish colony in Delaware. Within a few years, he resigned that office and returned to New York. In 1664, he was appointed sheriff of Kingston. By 1680, he was a deputy-mayor of New York City. Here he further accumulated his wealth. He bought land and built sailing ships, warehouses, flour mills and a brewery, becoming one of the city's largest wholesale merchants. There are still two streets in New York City named after him, William Street and Beekman Street. William married Catherine (or Catalina) De Boogh of New York on September 25, 1649, and with her had six sons—Hendrickus, Gerardus (from whom Franklin Delano Roosevelt is said to descend), Johannes, Jacobus, Wilhelmus and Martinus—and two daughters, Maria and Catherine.

(JUDGE) HENDRICKUS "HENRY" BEEKMAN (1652–1716), his oldest son, came to Esopus in 1663–64 with his father and apparently stayed. He was a successful businessman who later became a county judge. He was also a member of the "First Assembly under authority of the British King," which met in New York City on April 9, 1691, representing Dutchess and Ulster Counties, and he held other offices throughout his life.[22]

On April 22, 1697, Judge Beekman obtained a Royal Patent from Lord Cornbury for the lands to be called Ryn Beck. The boundaries were ambiguous, so on June 25, 1703, he obtained a better defined, broader patent. This second one brought with it some disputes, as it covered all the land in Kipsbergen, which was already in the hands of other patent holders (Artsen, Roosa, Elton and Kip), and some of the lands held by Peter Schuyler to the north. His Rhinebeck patent was one of two land patents he received at the same time. The other, a much larger one, covered the entire southeast corner of Dutchess County, including what are now the towns of Beekman, Pawling, Dover, Union Vale and LaGrange. Judge Henry Beekman never lived in Rhinebeck or Dutchess County, but he was active there. By 1703, he was surveying his property and had forced the routing of the Post Road through his patent. Two years later, he conveyed land to Traphagen and then to others. By 1710, he negotiated for new land and then set up a boat dock, gristmill and sawmill in Vanderburgh Cove on the falls of the Landsman Kill.[23] By 1715, he settled the Palatines, a displaced group of German settlers, on his land. Before he passed away, he was likely planning the mills on the flats (which came circa 1719).

Judge Beekman, a lifelong Kingston resident, married Joanna Lopers and had four children: William, who died in Holland at age eighteen; Henry Jr., who married Janet Livingston, daughter of Robert, the nephew of Robert, the "Lord of the Manor," the wealthy owner of the Livingston property just north of Dutchess County; Catryntie, or Catherine, who married John Rutsen and had four children, of which the Suckleys are descendants; and Cornelia, who married Gilbert Livingston, son of Robert, and had fourteen children. On May 6, 1713, Judge Beekman deeded his Dutchess County property to his son (though this transaction was not officially recorded).[24]

(COLONEL) HENRY BEEKMAN JR. (1687–1776) was a resident of Rhinebeck and a significant figure in its history. Account books show he was a prosperous businessman, managing the estate's rents, commerce, banking and other activities. By a land exchange, Colonel Beekman acquired the circa 1700 Kip House in Kipsbergen, and this became his home. A New York State historical marker on the ruins calls it the Kip-Beekman-Heermance House. He enlarged and improved the house and lived there until his death at age eighty-eight. Henry Beekman was listed as the colonel on the list of "Militie Officers &c &c of Dutchess County Viz to 21 Dece'r 1737."[25] In 1721, he married Janet Livingston, who died in 1724 at the early age of twenty-one. With her, he had two children: a son who died in infancy and a daughter, Margaret, who became the family matriarch. In 1728 (or 1726), he married Gertrude Van Cortlandt (another Livingston relative) and had no other children. With Henry's generation, the name of Beekman ended for this branch of the family. There is an old tradition recited by Smith that Colonel Beekman's grave is in the Reformed Dutch Church Cemetery and that the new (circa 1808) edifice was built over his grave.[26] Beekman had given this property to the community in 1730 to build the church on.

MARGARET BEEKMAN LIVINGSTON (1724–1800), the colonel's surviving daughter, married her cousin (Judge) Robert R. Livingston, the grandson of the "Lord of the Manor" and patentee, in 1742. In 1775, Margaret's life changed dramatically. Within a seven-month span, her father-in-law, father and husband all passed away, leaving her as the proprietress of a large part of the two Beekman patents, as well as a share of the Livingstons' land and their family home, Clermont.[27] Two years later, in 1777, the British burned her estate down. She rebuilt and endured. With her husband, Robert, she had eleven children. One died young, but the other ten all grew to become prominent citizens. A daughter, Janet (born 1744), married General Richard Montgomery, a respected officer who died tragically in the Revolutionary War trying to capture Quebec. Janet built the Rhinebeck mansion known today as Grasmere and was a prominent landholder, eventually owning the mills in Rhinebeck Flatts. Janet's later home was the estate now called Montgomery Place. Margaret's eldest son, Robert R. (born 1747), was "Chancellor" Livingston, then the highest judicial officer in New York State, who administered the oath of office to George Washington on the balcony of Federal Hall on Wall Street. He was on the committee that drafted the Declaration of Independence, he was minister to France and he negotiated the Louisiana Purchase. Robert also was the financial backer of Robert Fulton's North River steamboat.

Other children include:

MARGARET, who was born 1749 and married Dr. Thomas Tillotson, a Revolutionary War surgeon. Prominent in the politics of the state, he repeatedly served as senator and twice was secretary of state. The couple built the estate Linwood in Rhinebeck.

HENRY BEEKMAN LIVINGSTON, born 1750, was a colonel in Revolutionary army, Fourth New York Regiment. He fought in Canada, Saratoga, Valley

Gilbert Stuart's circa 1795 painting of Margaret Beekman Livingston. The original hangs in the Clermont State Historical Site. *Used with permission of the New York State Office of Parks, Recreation and Historic Preservation.*

Forge, Monmouth and Quaker Hill, Rhode Island. He took residence at the Kip-Heermance-Beekman house and married Nancy Shippen.

CATHERINE, born 1752, was wife of Reverend Freeborn Garrettson, one of the fathers of the Methodist Church. They built the Rhinebeck estate known as Wildercliff.

JOHN R., born 1754, was a merchant in New York City.

GERTRUDE, born 1757, was the wife of Morgan Lewis, general in both the Revolutionary War and the War of 1812. He was also a frequent member of the legislature, attorney general, chief justice, governor of the state and founder of Rhinebeck's Common Schools. The (later) Lewis mansion was on the site of the Odgen Mills mansion in Staatsburg.

JOANNA, born 1759, was the wife of Peter R. Livingston, a prominent politician. He was descended from Robert Livingston Jr. in the fourth generation. They later purchased and resided at Grasmere.[28]

ALIDA, born 1760, married General John Armstrong, U.S. senator, minister to France and secretary of war to President Madison. They built Rokeby, and their daughter was grandmother to John Jacob Astor IV of Rhinebeck.

EDWARD, born 1764, distinguished himself as a lawyer and statesman. He was secretary of state under President Jackson, minister to France, author of the Civil Code of Louisiana and once mayor of New York. He inherited all the land on the Rhinebeck Flats from his sister, Janet Montgomery, and later resided at Montgomery Place. His papers, originally kept at Montgomery Place, form the basis of the Princeton University archive collection.

All of these except Robert R., the chancellor, and John R. were at some period of their lives residents of Rhinebeck and occupants of lands inherited from their mother.[29] Margaret's portrait is an iconic image in the Hudson Valley. A copy still hangs proudly in the old Pewter Room (to the left of the lobby) of the Beekman Arms.

The Livingston family is descended from Robert Livingston (1654–1728) of Scotland, who was granted an extensive patent for lands that covered almost the entire lower part of Columbia County, just north of Dutchess. His property became the "Manor of Livingston." Robert married Alida (Schuyler) Van Rensselaer, with whom he had nine children. Many of their children and grandchildren married into the Beekman and other leading families.

CHAPTER 2

The Albany Post Road

It began as a matter of necessity. With settlements 150 miles apart in New York City and Albany, communication, trade and official travel were impossible by boat or ship when the river froze. Above Poughkeepsie, the river was often solid or filled with ice. John Adams, traveling in this area, wrote to his wife, Abigail:

> Poughkeepsie, 19 January, 1777.
> There is too much ice in Hudson's river to cross it in ferry boats, and too little to cross it without, in most places, which has given us the trouble of riding up the Albany road, as far as this place, where we expect to go over on the ice, but if we should be disappointed here, we must go up as far as Esopus, about fifteen miles further. This, as well as Fishkill, is a pretty village. We are almost wholly among the Dutch.[30]

The first impulse of the early settlers was to investigate the trails already blazed through the wilderness. Though no early maps show the native trails, this was the domain of the Lenape (the Wappinger and Wiccopee tribes in this region), and the trails that existed up and down the river likely were forged by them or their predecessors generations ago. Since they were not planned by surveyors or engineers, they often took circuitous routes following geological features and paths of least resistance. By the time the Dutch and English arrived, they were likely in poor condition, as the local population using them had been decimated by disease. Smallpox struck the area in both the early and late 1600s. Change was coming, as once colorfully described by author Nathaniel Hawthorne:

> *The forest-track, trodden more and more by the hob-nailed shoes of these sturdy and ponderous Englishmen, has now a distinctness which it never could have acquired from the light tread of a hundred times as many moccasins…it goes onward from one clearing to another, here plunging into a shadowy strip of woods, there open to the sunshine, but everywhere showing a decided line, along which the human interests have begun to hold their career.*[31]

Morse and others suggest postal service carried by natives began sometime between 1672 and 1705, but it is difficult finding support for this claim. More than likely, if it did occur, it was winter only; the summer mail run was done by river sloop, taking four to eight days to reach Albany.

Much has been written about the road's more famous cousin east, the Boston Post Road. On this road, the first mail service was established in January 1673, and the first "official" stagecoach service started in 1783. At least half a dozen scholarly books cover this road's history. For the Albany Post Road, published history is lacking. In the *28*th *Annual Report of the American Scenic and Historic Preservation Society, 1922–23* presented to the state legislature, it was noted, "There are few persons who know very much about that one time important artery of travel and trade, that connected a thriving city at one end of it with the capital of the State at the other."[32] One account does exist. In 1905, writer Charles Hines took a stroll from New York City to Albany and recounted his contemporary tale in his book *The New York and Albany Post Road*. As a historical reference, it is brief and lacks detail. It mentions the "hotel corner" as the start of a side excursion to Rhinecliff, but nothing else. Few other taverns along the way are noticed. Steven Jenkins's brilliant 1911 book *The Greatest Street in the World* is also a tale of the Albany Post Road, but its primary focus is New York City (Broadway). Barely any mention is made of Rhinebeck, and there is nothing on the BA. A few years later in 1926, Elise Lathrop does a jaunt down the Post Road in her classic volume *Early American Inns and Taverns*, but her book is undocumented and generally draws on her own observations and on oral histories. The BA is mentioned, and she offers some useful contemporary remarks, but for the history, it is not reliable.

Much like the BA, the road's lack of a detailed written history is no surprise. The river was the first choice for northern travel. Stages initially were expensive,

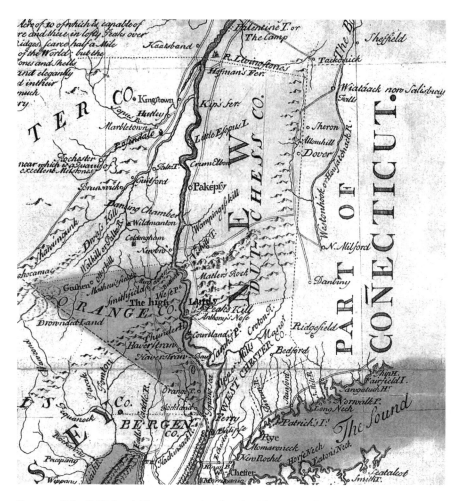

Excerpt of the 1749 Lewis Evans map showing the Albany Post Road. One of the earliest maps known to exist showing its full extent. *Library of Congress.*

and transit was difficult through the remote, mountainous highlands. Notorious "highwaymen" lurked in Westchester County and preyed on travelers, making early travel hazardous at times. Upstate itself was a mix of sparse, remote farmland and dense forest—seemingly much less interesting than where all the action was on Manhattan Island. The "lore" surrounding the Albany Post Road farther north was just slow to develop.

Remarkably, the earliest published map showing the complete road northward to Albany does not seem to appear until 1749. This is the Lewis Evans map, covering "PENSILVANIA, NEW-JERSEY, NEW-YORK, And the THREE DELAWARE COUNTIES." Given its small scale, detail is omitted, and only town names are provided. A famous 1715 Herman Moll map shows the Post Road to Boston (and one in New Jersey to Philadelphia), but not the road to Albany. Most of the surviving larger maps produced during this time period seemingly were made for purposes other than as road maps. It was not until the American Revolution that serviceable travel maps were required.

THE ROAD NORTH FROM NEW YORK CITY

Both Post Roads, together at this point, started at city hall in lower Manhattan. From here, the road ran up the island two miles (here called Bowery Lane) before splitting into two separate paths—Bloomingdale Road to the west (following the old Wickquasgeck Indian Path) and Kingsbridge Road, or the Post Road, toward the east (these names were being used by 1776). This split was near present-day Madison Park on Twenty-Third Street. After

View of the Tavern on the Road to King's Bridge, Near Fort Washington. Charles Motte, lithographer, 1825. This was near the present George Washington Bridge and shows the remote wilderness that once was upper Manhattan. *Courtesy of the American Antiquarian Society.*

running through this sparsely settled farm country, both roads reconnected near McGowan's Tavern/Pass, now the northeast tip of Central Park, and continued north together another five miles.[33] It then crossed the Spuyten Duyvil Creek into what is now the Bronx. Originally, this crossing was a ford (called "the wading place" by the natives), but by 1653, a bridge was built. This area came to be called "King's Bridge."[34] From here, the path turned east through a marsh and then divided, with one fork going over a hill to Williamsbridge and on to Boston, the other turning north and west, becoming part of the Albany Post Road "opened to the Saw-kill [Yonkers] about 1669."[35] It was a full day's journey (fifteen miles) to get from lower Manhattan to the northern tip of the island; near here, the early traveler found his first rest.

MAKING OF THE ROAD NORTH

On June 19, 1703, the Colonial Assembly passed "AN ACT for the Laying out Regulateing Clearing and preserving Publick Comon highways thro'out this Colony," setting out the requirement for a usable road north.[36] Among other things, it provided for a highway "to Extend from Kings Bridge in the County of West Chester thro' the same County of West Chester[,] Dutchess County and the County of Albany of the breadth of Four Rods English Measure at the Least to be Continue and remain for ever the Publick Comon General Road and Highway from King Bridge aforesaid to the Ferry at Crawlew over against the City of Albany."

The act further provided that the owners of the townships through which any road ran should clear, mend and repair the road, and it appointed commissioners in several counties, including Dutchess. The commissioners' first duty was to see that the road should be "laid out Ascertained and declared" within eighteen months after the publication of the act.

Baltus Van Clifft, Johannus Tarbus and Robert Livingston were selected for Dutchess County and specifically named in this act. Morse adds, "In Rhinebeck, Judge Beekman fixed the route, and the road is entirely on his patent. Naturally it should have been laid out near the river. He forced it over 'clay hill' and east of the two kills. This brought it through 'the flatts' and is the reason why the present village is two miles back from the river."[37]

To maintain the road, a system developed of "working the roads" in the early eighteenth century. The Highway Act of October 30, 1708, specifically established a requirement for each "freeholder and inhabitant" (or their servant) to "work and Labour for the clearing, leveling and amending the same High Ways not exceeding Six days in the year under Penalty of three shillings for each Day every person shall neglect or refuse such service."[38]

MILESTONE MARKERS

To mark distances (from New York City), price out mail service and help with navigation, mile markers were set in place on the western side of the road. The first ones date to 1769 along the Post Road in Manhattan.[39] Milestones further up the Post Road were set in place in accordance with the "Act to Regulate Highways," passed on March 21, 1797. It states: "The superintendents of highways of the counties respectively, out of any monies which may come into their hands by virtue of this act, shall causes proper stones or posts to be erected by one of the sides of the post road leading from Kingsbridge to Albany...at a distance of one mile from each other."[40]

Any person defacing the signs faced a hefty three-pound (later ten-dollar) penalty.[41] Various towns and counties took to encasing, replacing and restoring the stones over the years. For the markers in Dutchess County, Franklin Roosevelt insisted the Dutchess County Historical Society take charge of preserving them by encasing each in a stone masonry enclosure, which it did during his tenure as president. (Milestone 86 is right in front of his Hyde Park home. This likely influenced his appreciation for these small monuments.) Rhinebeck has seven red sandstone markers, mile markers 95–101. All seven still exist, though some seem to have been moved slightly over time, and several are in rough shape. Of the forty in Dutchess County, twenty-eight still exist.[42]

There was no distinction between the Boston Post Road being called the "Kings Highway" and the Albany Post Road being the "Kings Road," as some suggest. Both terms are used interchangeably in historical documents when referring to the Albany Post Road. All major thoroughfares were accorded the same tribute to the king. (Even West Market Street in Rhinebeck is labeled as "Kings High Way" on a 1770 plot plan.)[43] Technically, 1702–14 was the reign of Queen Anne, so the roads must have been the "Queen's Highway" before they became the king's.

EXPANSION OF THE ROAD

Hostilities between the warring nations of France and Great Britain—particularly through the Queen Anne period, followed by the rule of George I (1714–1727), George II (1727–1760, with the French and Indian War from 1754–1763) and then George III (1760–1820, during the Revolution and War of 1812)—necessitated the movement of troops and a great amounts of supplies. Anything not transported by ship was moved by wagon up this road. The road was also the primary paths for drovers moving livestock between fields and market. All this use led to trampled conditions and a constant need for road improvements. When commercial stage travel began in 1785, both necessity and legislation brought the road to a higher level of serviceability, though this took years. Eventually, parts of the road were rerouted to improve travel efficiency and safety. The circa 1804 Highland Turnpike, for example, shunted travel around the Hudson Highlands. South of Rhinebeck, the Post Road originally ran through Staatsburg. Between 1933 and 1934, it was rerouted slightly east of its historic path.[44] A little farther north of this reroute, it was expanded to four lanes.

After the French and Indian War, the Post Road was used by both sides during the American Revolution. Map makers for the king and for George Washington and his colonial army set about mapping the route. John Montrésor, an officer in King George's Royal Engineers Corps, produced a famous 1775 map of New York, as did Claude Joseph Sauthier in 1776. The most detailed of these Revolution-era maps was done by Surveyor General Robert Erskine and his assistant Simeon De Witt in 1779 for George Washington. Erskine's mapset shows mile-by-mile detail of what was on the Post Road at the time, down to taverns and mills. Mapping from Albany southward, Erskine's mile designations are opposite the more commonly seen northbound milestones.

Ten years later in 1789, following (and directly copying) the Erskine map, mapmaker and entrepreneur Christopher Colles produced another publication that mapped the Post Road north. Colles's *A Survey of the Roads of the United States of America* was America's first road atlas.[45] It is often cited, and it is so highly regarded that it currently is on display at the Library of Congress as part of its exhibit "Books that Shaped America." Interestingly, neither Erskine nor Colles shows a hotel or tavern where the Beekman Arms is located. Both highlight "Trimpers T" (a tavern, by virtue of the symbol on Colles's map and Erskine's use of *T* for tavern) in

Rhinebeck Flats. Using the scale of the Colles map, this tavern seems to have been located right across and a few feet north from present-day Platt Avenue.[46] A will in the probate court records dated 3/13/1789, exists for this Jacob Trimper. He calls himself "innholder," and the principal asset he gives to his heirs is his "brewhouse and brewing implements."[47] A Jacob Tremper (but not Trimper) appears on the county tax lists from June 1759 to 1778, so it is quite possible "Trimper" and "Tremper" were just used interchangeably.[48] The Tremper family seemed to be one of wealth and influence in town (typically the type of people who were tavern owners; indeed, two separate generations came to be landlords of the BA). Colles says of his maps: "Each page containing a delineation of near 12 miles of road...and particularly specifying all the cross roads and streams of water which intersect it, the names of the most noted inhabitants of the houses contiguous to or in view of the road, the churches and other public buildings; the taverns, blacksmith shops, mills and every object which occurs to render it a useful and entertaining work."

From this description, one wonders why he did not pick up on the second structure Erskine notes near the intersection. The unlabeled house inside the fork, possibly the BA or possibly another old stone house known to exist near here, appears to stay through both maps. It is impossible to provide a definitive answer. What is very clear is that Colles simply copied and cleaned up Erskine's map for republication. It is not original work, as it is spot-on identical to that of Erskine. Colles took on an ambitious project, mapping from Williamsburg, Virginia, all the way to Albany (with a detour out to Stratford, Connecticut), so he likely took shortcuts where he thought he could. He may not have even come through town to map it (he lived in Kingston until 1777, so perhaps he felt he did not need to do so). Since his 1789 map is identical to the 1779 map, it also erroneously implies nothing at all changed in ten years, except that a sizable building (possibly the BA) somehow disappeared.[49] It is interesting that neither map identifies any "noted inhabitants" in the houses near the intersection.

With respect to the BA not being labeled as a tavern, the only possible explanation is that it was not yet one by 1779, and possibly not even by 1789, and perhaps it was just a house and/or store (which neither mapmaker noted). The presumed owner at the time, Everardus Bogardus, lists himself as a merchant and not as innkeeper, just as the first owner (Cole) did.

The landscape changed significantly through the years as the population grew and businesses prospered, failed and changed hands. In 1714, all of

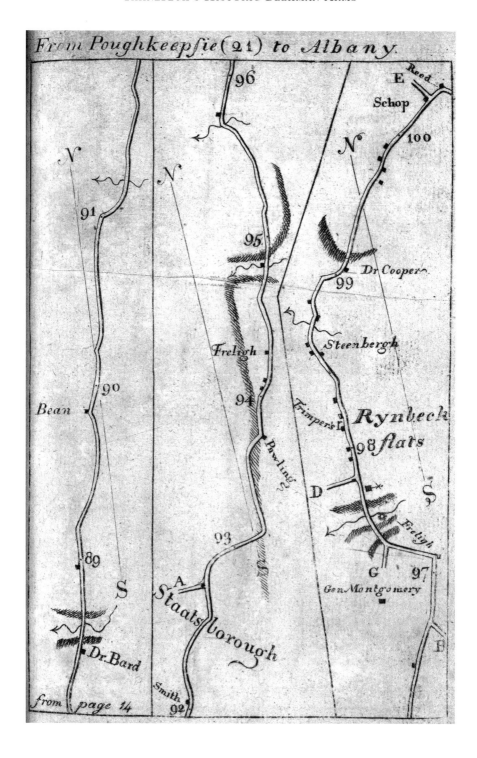

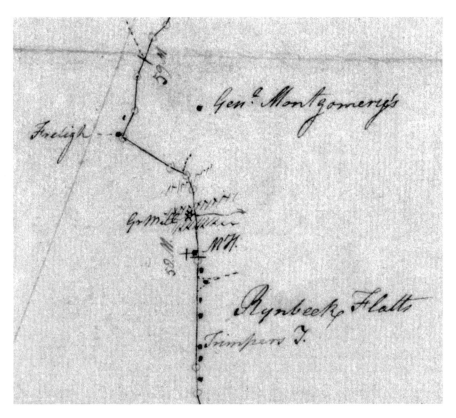

Erskine's 1779 "93R" map (excerpt above, south is to the top) and Colles's 1789 map (previous page, north is to the top). On Erskine's map, you see a gristmill, a meetinghouse, West Market Street/the Sepasco Trail forking into the Post Road (just above "Rhinebeck Flats") and two dots, one possibly the structure that later becomes the Beekman Arms. The Colles map is nearly an identical copy (though shown stretching from Hyde Park to Hook Road near 9/9G). Trimper's Tavern is the prominent stopping point in town. "D" is West Market Street on the Colles map. *Erskine map courtesy of the New York Historical Society; Colles map courtesy of the David Rumsey Map Collection, www.davidrumsey.com (the entire map book can be found here, this is map 21).*

Dutchess County had 445 "souls," including 29 slaves. By 1790, Rhinebeck alone had 3,662 residents, including 421 slaves.[50]

Eighteen postwar years after Erskine came through, the New York legislature mandated that towns submit to the surveyor-general local maps so he could compile these and create a detailed map of the entire state. Local surveyor Alexander Thompson was tasked to produce one for Rhinebeck, which he finished in late 1797 and published in January 1798. His richly detailed map shows stunning changes, as the Post Road

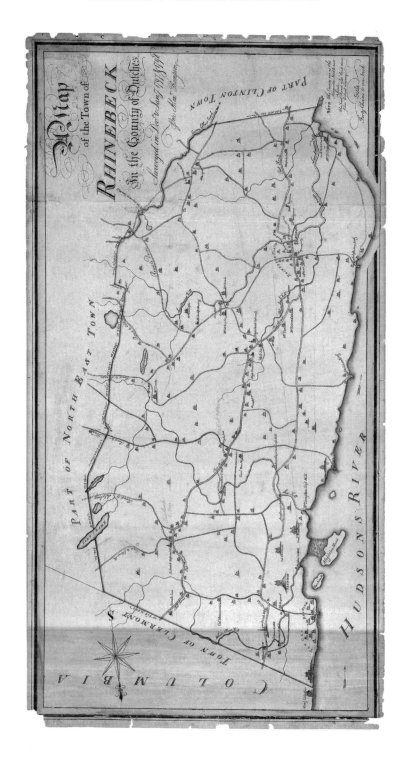

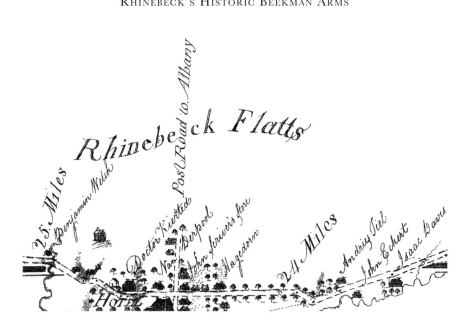

Above: Excerpt from "Map of the Turnpike Road." North is to the top. The BA is labeled as "Hotel" on the middle bottom, the first ever notation of this property as a business. The map extends from the river all the way to the Connecticut border to the right (though ripped at this end). The 1806 mapmaker notes in the New York State Archives (Cockburn Papers, box 9, folder 10) call the hotel "Jackway's Hottel." *Map: DCRD map #28.*

Opposite: "Map of the Town of Rhinebeck, In the County of Dutches~, Surveyed in Dec & Jan 1797 and 1798, per Alexr Thompson." One of four copies of this map. There is no mention of Bogardus, and "Montgomery Lodge" is a prominent label for the BA. *Courtesy of the New York State Archives.*

appears populated with numerous homes, taverns (eight now in the greater village area), mills and other features of the area. The map is somewhat illustrative, as the scale of the houses and their proximity to one another is not practical. Also, no businesses besides inns are generally shown. It is, however, a remarkable historical document. Thompson subsequently copied his map at least three other times over the next two years, and each has subtle differences.[51] With respect to the BA, none clearly note it as a tavern.

By 1802, the dirt path referred to as the Sepasco (or Sepascot) Trail running east–west in town (now Rhinecliff Road and West and East Market Streets) was used as the foundation of a new road to Connecticut called the Ulster and Salisbury Turnpike. This road was part of a greater turnpike route that ran from the Susquehanna River in the vicinity of the town of

41

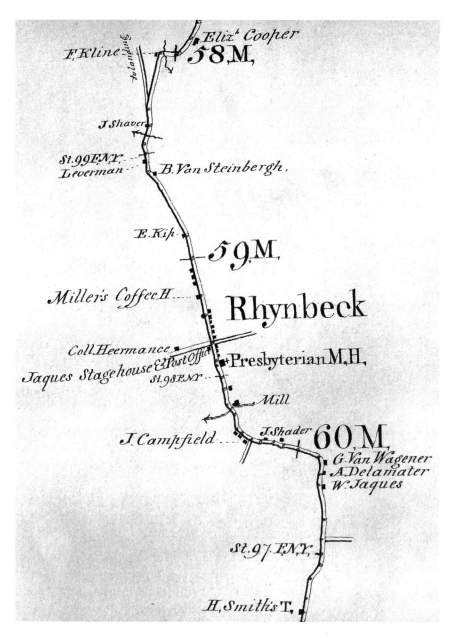

Excerpt from the twenty-two-foot-long *A Map of the Post Road, between the Cities of ALBANY and NEW YORK, Surveyed by Order of the Corporation of the City of Albany in September 1810 by John Randel Junr.* Mile measurements are from Albany and do not match the milestones on the ground. Note also the name W. Jaques near the bottom, possibly his home. *Courtesy of the Albany County Hall of Records.*

Jerico (Bainbridge today, near, surprisingly, Binghamton) to the Connecticut state line at Salisbury.[52] Salisbury, circa 1741, was the seat of an important iron ore industry that operated from the Revolution all the way to the 1920s. The route through Rhinebeck to the Hudson was therefore a somewhat significant (but very long) commerce route. A map of this road was produced in 1802. On it, the BA is shown quite notably as a "Hotel." The 1922 bronze plaque on the BA's front lawn commemorating the road mentions this was a route used by Connecticut pioneers to settle in their new home in western New York.[53]

In 1810, mapmaker John Randel Jr. produced a remarkable twenty-two-foot-long map of the entire Albany Post Road. This map shows less detail, but understandably so, as he covered much more ground than Thompson. (Randel is famous for laying out the road grid system in New York City.) On Randel's map, we see the BA noted as "Jaques Stagehouse." Trimper's seems to have turned into a coffeehouse. By 1810, these appear to be the two most notable taverns in town. (Note also that only a single structure is shown near the BA corner, just as the Colles map illustrates.)

In 1829, the David Burr New York county maps came out showing the entire Post Road. No taverns or stage stops are noted due to its small scale (though surprisingly, down in Cold Spring, "Warrens" can be seen on the map). By 1867, the famous and ubiquitous F.W. Beers Atlas collection came out for New York. These maps begin to show the impact of the railroads through the various cities and towns. Commerce routes clearly had shifted, and many taverns had been replaced by "modern" hotels. Gray's Atlas collection in 1876 soon followed. The Rhinebeck Hotel appears on both of these maps. Though two miles from the railroad, it was well established by that point in history and was surrounded by a thriving community. Unlike many old taverns, the railroad was not pushing it aside.

Here on the Post Road and the road to the river, the local stagecoach and transport wagon business was still running strong. People and products—such as slate, milk, food stocks, violets, produced goods and raw materials—coming from all directions needed to get to the docks through town. This continued by horse and wagon until the early 1900s when the automobile was first introduced—the first change in travel means in some 275 years.

This transition from horse to horseless travel is best illustrated on a series of maps produced by the Sanborn Map Company. The Sanborn Company mapped towns across the country for fire liability insurance purposes. Maps of Rhinebeck exist from at least 1886 to 1941. On these

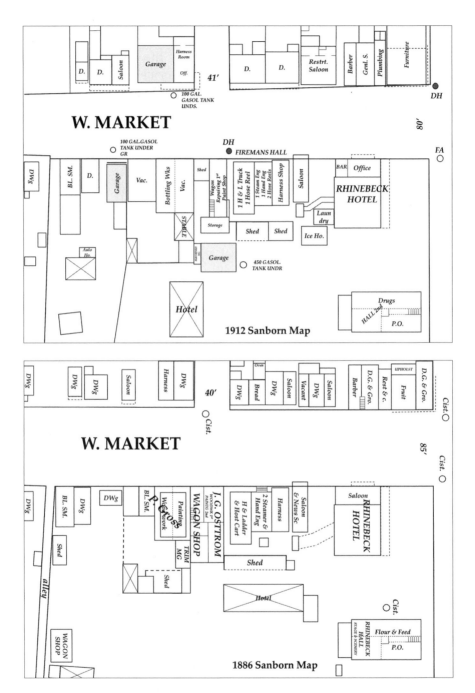

Sanborn maps from 1886 and 1912 showing changes from the horse-drawn to horseless era. Maps exist for 1886, 1895, 1900, 1905, 1912, 1923 and 1941. They also provide a visual history of the violet industry's explosive growth and contraction in town. *Courtesy of the New York Public Library. Facsimiles used for clarity.*

Rhinebeck, N.Y. Drawn & published by L.R. Burleigh, 1890. Excerpt showing the area around the Rhinebeck Hotel. In 1890, the BA was owned by Catherine Fulmer and managed by Lorenzo Decker. *Library of Congress*

maps, you can see the remarkable changes from the horse-drawn era to the automotive age. Blacksmith, wagon and tack shops surrounding the BA were gradually replaced by garages.[54]

CHAPTER 3

Days of Stage Travel, Eighty Years Later

After the Revolutionary War, the country's dirt roads became safer and easier to travel. Technology improvements of the day, such as the use of leather straps as springs (called thorough braces), were also beginning to make wheeled vehicles such as stagecoaches a little more bearable. The economy was expanding, and the growing population was on the move. To meet the rising demand for trade and mobility, a commercial stage business

Mail-Coach Changing Horses, from the October 1855 *Ballou's Pictorial Drawing-Room Companion*. The inn in the background looks remarkably similar to the 1849 sketch of the Rhinebeck Hotel.

soon emerged on the Post Road. This business existed for some seventy years—from the issuance of the first Albany Post Road stage license in June 1785 to just after the railroad started in roughly 1855. Rhinebeck, ideally situated a day's travel from Albany to the north and Peekskill to the south (with a few horse-team changes in between), was a noted overnight travel stop in several early advertisements.[55] Though the BA was not the only stage office in town, its prominent location, its sole notation on maps, its spaciousness, its surrounding stables and the fact that a notable landlord, William Jacques, ran the hotel for many years all lead one to believe it played a dominant role in the area. Since the BA came into prominence during this time period, it is only fitting to add details of this once important but now virtually forgotten era to the story.

THE FIRST STAGE LICENSE AND EARLY TAVERNS

For the months the river was navigable and before steam ships, early water travel was often slow and monotonous. With luck, it could take as little as two days to reach Albany (particularly in the summer when the south wind prevailed and the tide was timed properly), but if the wind was not blowing, it could take up to eight days. In stormy conditions, particularly when squalls hit, travel could become treacherous. Being caught in a small craft in the middle of one of these was a real risk to travelers.

Passenger vessels had sleeping quarters and some type of meal service. These boats could dock at night if they wanted to sacrifice time, but accommodations were likely incomparable to that of the better roadside taverns, with tables full of fresh food and bars filled with inviting spirits (albeit, a rough trip might need to be endured for these). For the wandering type, there was just far less adventure involved in river travel and much more experience (and business) to be gained from traveling the countryside. Rivers also only reached port cities, and these were bound up four months out of the year by ice. All of these reasons, as well as the never-ending desire to profit, prompted the establishment of a land-based stage business.

Initially, both the demand for stage service and the operational risk involved were unknown. Potential operators were also worried about competition easily entering the fray once someone had figured out how to profitably operate such a service. To entice someone to step forward, the State of New York offered the incentive of a ten-year exclusive license.

Three tavern keepers—Isaac Van Wyck of Fishkill, John Kinney of Kinderhook and Talmadge Hall of New York City—partnered together and were granted the first license in June 1785. In exchange for the license, the tavern keepers had to have two stages running twice a week, and they had to agree to reach Albany or New York in three days. Apparently this was never an issue, as business was so good the tavern keepers increased the schedule to three trips a week, and they figured out how to make the trip in only two days. As the business grew, Van Wyck, Kinney and Talmadge took on other partners, particularly tavern keepers situated where horse-team changes could be made. In his book *Stagecoach East*, Oliver W. Holmes briefly describes the trip:

> *When on the two day schedule, the stages left their respective terminals at five o'clock in the morning, the one setting out from the ferry landing that was opposite the city of Albany, and the other from Cape's Tavern in New York City. Passengers for Albany stopped for breakfast at ten o'clock at Kinney's Tavern in Kinderhook, reached* **Rhinebeck** *about two o'clock for dinner, and passed on in the afternoon through Poughkeepsie to Fishkill, where Van Wyck gave them supper and lodging. Passengers from New York, meanwhile, had breakfast at Hall's Tavern on Washington Heights, where passengers in the Boston stage also breakfasted, dined at Mandeville's in Peekskill, and also arrived to sup and lodge in Van Wyck's. The stages exchanged passengers the next morning, and each traveled back on the road it came, observing the same stops.*[56]

Arthur Weise's 1884 book, *The History of the City of Albany*, reveals more:

> *Kinney, Van Wyck, and Hall were to provide at least two good and properly covered coaches, drawn by four able horses, and were not to charge more than four pence per mile for the conveyance of a passenger, who was to be allowed the free transportation of fourteen pounds of baggage. The stages were to depart once each week from the two cities unless prevented by the bad condition of the roads, or some unavoidable accident. The fare, in the summer of 1794, from Albany to New York, was $7.25; in the following winter, $8. The price in the winter of 1796 was increased to $10, but in the following spring it was reduced to $6.*[57]

A 1905 article in *The Outlook* magazine titled "Along the Hudson in Stage-Coach Days" by R.P.H. Vail has even more to add: "Stops for a part of the

Taverns Along the Post Road, Colles, 1789 (with nearest mile marker)	
Start at City Hall	
2 Devenport (Lower Manhattan)	47 Lent's Tavern
5 Dean's Tavern	48 Griffin's Tavern (near rd to Peekskill Ldg)
5 Grierson's Tavern	48 Birdsall's Tavern (near rd to Peekskill Ldg)
5 Adamson's Tavern	50 Dusenbury's Tavern (just before Peekskill Cr)
8 Legget's Tavern (near McGowen house)	54 (55) Traver's Tavern (near Continental Village)
9 Day's Tavern	56 (57) Roger's Tavern (Philipstown)
9 Neil's Tavern	61 Mead's Tavern
11 Waldran Tavern (Near Ft Washington)	63 Weeks' Tavern
11 Englehart Tavern (Near Ft. Washington)	66 VanWyck's (just before Fishkill) Tavern
13 Myer's Taverns (1m just before KB)	68 VanWyck's Tavern in Fishkill
14 Hyatt's Tavern (just before Kingsbridge)	68 Rapalje's Tavern in Fishkill
14 Halsey's Tavern (just over creek)	72 Shute's Tavern (near Wap. Kill Landing)
19 Hunt's Tavern (near Philips's)	75 Lawson's Tavern (other side of creek)
22 Archer Tavern	78 Fraer's Tavern (near Rd to Lewis Ferry)
25 Dusenbury's Tavern (Dobbs Ferry)	81 Myer's Tavern (just before Pokpk bridge)
30 Covenhoven Tavern	81/82 Kelsey's (downtown Poughkeepsie)
34 Lefter's Tavern	81/82 Hendricks & Pools (downtown Pok.)
34 Drake's Tavern	98 Trimper's Tavern (Rhinebeck Flats)
36 Ward's Tavern	102 Tater's Tavern (just before Red Hook)
39 Delezenne Tavern (N of Croton River)	106 Thomas's Tavern (Upper Red Hook)
40 Merrit's Tavern	130 Fosbury's Tavern (before Kinderhook)

Listing of taverns (and possibly stagecoach stops) that existed between 1779 and 1789, as shown in the Colles Atlas from New York City to Albany. *Complete map set on davidrumsey.com (search "Colles 1789").*

night were made at Rhinebeck and Peekskill, where the taverns were said to be exceptionally good, but the sleeping accommodations of which were so limited that two men, though strangers, were generally put in one bed." Vail continues: "In the early years of the last century, a continuous road was opened on the west side of the river by way of Catskill, Kingston, Newburg, Goshen, and Hackensack, which, though even more winding than the east side, soon had its line of stages. Rivalry between competing lines soon resulted in quickened speed, cheaper fares, increased misery to passengers, and a demoralization of equipment." In 1816, "two days and one night were painfully disposed of in the journey," and in February 1820, "the east side company boasted of having made the shortest land passage from Albany to New York—in fifteen hours." Vail also describes how the river, once sections were solidly frozen over, became a stage highway using sleds and shanty taverns in the 1830–40s.[58]

In 1835, the conditions and business practices in the New York stage industry changed dramatically when Charles L. Beach and his father, Erastus, "secured proprietary control of the stage and mail runs" on both sides of the Hudson, as well as the line between Catskill and Ithaca (this run was said to be the most expeditious and popular route to the "Great West"). This merger was the most famous business consolidation of the day. The Beaches were already running a highly efficient and much respected stage business in Catskill. They also owned the popular Catskill Mountain House and ran vacation stages to it. Timetables, meals, equipment, horses and services were all improved and standardized under their leadership, and within a year, "public patronage had increased threefold."[59] (In 1827, the very reliable and comfortable Abbot-Downing Concord Coach was also first introduced. This improvement undoubtedly helped all operators.)

Christopher Colles makes note of the forty-two Post Road taverns in existence in 1789 (or more likely 1779) between Albany and New York's City Hall. His atlas came out just as the stage business was taking off. Quite understandably, stage owners, innkeepers and travelers were constantly negotiating for better terms and looking for ways to improve their travel experience. As these agreements and conditions changed over time, so did the tavern landscape. Some taverns prospered; some did not. Generally speaking, those that did were spaced fifteen to twenty miles apart from the last good one—the length of time before horses needed to be changed. Only Thomas' Tavern in Red Hook (now a private home) on this list can still be found. (The surviving Cornelius/Isaac Van Wyck's Homestead historic site in Fishkill makes no claim of having been a tavern.) The other taverns on his map all appear to be long gone, and none was prominent enough to leave a lasting legacy. Thirteen years later, the BA would show up, first briefly as Potter's, then as Jacques'. It remains the only early stage hotel still operating and likely still in existence.

RHINEBECK'S LOCAL STAGE LINE HISTORY

There exists no narrative of what the local shorter-haul business was like, but some scattered details are recorded to offer a sense of how this industry operated in town. A New York State historic marker for Peter Pultz's Tavern a few hundred yards up East Market Street from the BA makes mention that this was the headquarters of the "Yellow Bird" stage line. Morse appears to be the source of this information when he provides the story of the Pultz Tavern in his book (this tavern was otherwise known as the Bowery and was destroyed by fire in 1960). Morse also mentions another stage line headquartered a few hundred feet from the BA: "Garden Street, then a road, was filled with stage barns. Marquardt's bakery was on the corner. A stage house adjoined it on the east, the Blue Bird line." Neither of these stage lines appears in any historical records, though the later stage house he refers to is the Wortz/Fraleigh livery stable pictured in this book. This period was somewhat contemporary to Morse in his youth, so it is quite possible he had firsthand knowledge of this business in town.

In addition to the Yellow Bird and Blue Bird lines in town, there appears to be another one: the Redbird line. From a September 5, 1908 *Rhinebeck Gazette* history article: "In winter—the Redbird and the Bluebird, the first having its stage house at Jacques tavern, the other at Pultz's, made stage hours interesting. Each had warm admirers. A blast from the stage horn called them forth. In summer, the steamboats and barges made regular trips." (Recorded history appears to be mixing some of these lines.)

Stage Routine

Typically, stagecoaches departed very early, hours before sunrise, and traveled ten miles or so before breakfast. The poet Longfellow, on his October 1862 ride west out of Boston to the Red Horse Tavern in Sudbury, famously commented on his early morning departure, saying, "The stage left Boston about 3 o'clock in the morning, reaching the Sudbury Tavern for breakfast, a considerable portion of the route being traveled in total darkness, and without you having the least idea who your traveling companion might be."[60]

Nathaniel Hawthorne writes similarly on a July 1838 stagecoach ride he took west out of Northhampton, Massachusetts:

> *Left Northhampton the next morning, between one and two o'clock. Three other passengers, whose faces were not visible for some hours; so we went on through unknown space, saying nothing, glancing forth sometimes to the gleam of the lanterns on wayside objects.*
>
> *How very desolate looks a forest when seen in this way,—as if, should you venture one step within its wild, tangled, many-stemmed, and dark-shadowed verge, you would inevitably be lost forever. Sometimes we passed a*

NEW-YORK AND ALBANY
MAIL STAGE,

LEAVES New-York every morning at 6 o'clock, lodges at Peekskill and Rhinebeck, and arrives in Albany on the third-day. Fare of each passenger through eight dollars, and 6d per mile for way passengers. For Seats apply to *William Vandervoort*, No. 48, corner of Courtland and Greenwich streets, New-York, and of *T. Witmore*, Albany

February 13 tf   POTTER, HYATT & Co.

LINE OF STAGES.

FOR the greater convenience of Travellers, and to avoid accidents, the proprietors of the above line of stages have determined to alter their time of starting, and in future, to perform the passage to and from Albany and New-York, altogether by day-light. To effect this arrangement,

THE DILIGENCE STAGE,

will, on *Monday*, the 22d inst. and every day thereafter, leave New-York at 6 o'clock in the morning, and perform the route in two days and an half—from New-York, will breakfast at Kingsbridge—lodge at Warren's in the Highlands—breakfast at Fishkill on the second day, lodge at Hudson, and arrive at Albany, at 12, on the third day.

Leave Albany about the same hour in the morning, breakfast at Kinderhook, lodge at Rhinebeck, breakfast at Poughkeepsie on the second day, lodge at Sing-Sing, and arrive in New-York at 12 o'clock on the third day.

THE MAIL STAGE

Will leave New-York, on Mondays, Wednesdays and Fridays, at 8 o'clock, A. M. and on Tuesdays, Thursdays and Saturdays, at 4 A. M. and will leave Albany every morning in the week, Sundays excepted, and will run through in two days; the number of Passengers will be limited to SIX, on Mail days.

Seats to be taken at the *STAGE-OFFICE*, No. 2, Green-Street, and Cande's Connecticut Coffee-House, Albany, and at No. 5, Cortlandt-Street, New-York; likewise at Henry Kelsey's, Poughkeepsie.

All Baggage, as usual, to be at the risk of the Owner.

I. Wetmore, Albany.	T. Goodyear, N. Y.
John B. Swan,	J. Hunt,
L. Baker,	H. Kelsey,
J. Campbell,	P. Cole,
T. Powell, & Co.	PROPRIETORS.

Albany, January 16, 1815.   6eptf

ALBANY MAIL STAGE

WILL commence running 3d December next; leaves Albany every morning at 3 o'clock, breakfast at Hudson, dine at Poughkeepsie;—breakfast at Singsing, dine in New-York. Returning, leaves New-York at half past 3, A. M. dine at Singsing, sup at Fishkill; breakfast at Rhinebeck, dine at Kinderhook; arrives at Albany at evening. 14lb. baggage gratis; 100 lb. baggage to pay the same as a passenger. All baggage at the risk of the owner.

DILIGENCE STAGE

Commences running 3d December next, as follows: Leaves Albany every morning at 5 o'clock, breakfast at Kinderhook, dine at Rhinebeck, lodge at Poughkeepsie ; leaves Poughkeepsie at 3 o'clock next morning, breakfast at Singsing, dine at Singsing, and sup in New-York Returning, leaves New-York at 4 o'clock, A. M. breakfast at Kingsbridge, dine at Peekskill, sup and lodge at Poughkeepsie ; leaves Poughkeepsie at 3 o'clock, breakfast at Rhinebeck, dine at Kinderhook, and sup in Albany. 14lb. baggage allowed gratis. 100lb. baggage to pay the same as a passenger. All baggage at the risk of the owner.

The subscribers have prepared good horses and carriages, careful and sober drivers, and will endeavor to make choice of the best houses on the road for accommodations. They will spare no pains to give their customers general satisfaction.

Apply for seats in the above line of stages at Nos. 1 and 5 Courtlandt-street, New-York, and No. 2 Green-street, Albany.

LEONARD BAKER & CO.	Albany
J. WETMORE,	Do
SWAN & CAMPBELL,	Do
PETER COLE,	Hudson.
HENRY KELSEY,	Poughkeepsie.
JOSEPH HUNT,	Singsing.
VAN RANST & GOODYEAR,	N York
THOMAS B. GATES,	Do

Nov 14

ALBANY STAGES,
THROUGH IN TWO DAYS.

DILIGENCE STAGE starts from No. 1 Courtlandt-street every morning at 4 o'clock ; lodges at Poughkeepsie, and arrives at Albany the next evening.

THE NEW LINE ACCOMMODATION STAGE, [through in three days,] will commence running this day—to start every other day at 9 o'clock in the morning, from No. 1 Courtland street—lodge at Peekskill & Rhinebeck, and arrive at Albany the third day.

For seats in the above named Stages, apply to THOMAS WHITFIELD, at the old established Stage Office, old No. 1 Courtlandt-st. second office from Broadway, New-York.

N. B. All goods and baggage at the risk of the owner.   LEONARD BAKER & CO.

P. S. Expresses sent to any part of the United States at the shortest notice, by
THOMAS WHITFIELD,
jy 19   No. 1 Courtlandt-st. New-York.

house, or rumbled through a village, stopping perhaps to arouse some drowsy postmaster, who appeared at the door in shirt and pantaloons, yawning, received the mail, returned it again, and was yawning when last seen. A few words exchanged among the passengers, as they roused themselves from their half-slumbers, or dreamy, slumber-like abstraction. Meantime dawn broke, our faces became partially visible, the morning air grew colder, and finally cloudy day came on. We found ourselves driving through quite a romantic country,...and rattled on at the rate of ten miles an hour. Breakfast between four and five,—newly caught trout, salmon, ham, boiled eggs, and other niceties,—truly excellent. A bunch of pickerel, intended for a tavern-keeper farther on, was carried by the stage-driver. The drivers carry a "time-watch" enclosed in a small wooden case, with a lock, so that it may be known in what time they perform their stages. They are allowed so many hours and minutes to do their work, and their desire to go as fast as possible, combined with that of keeping their horses in good order, produces about a right medium.[61]

Stagecoaches carried at least six passengers with typically fourteen pounds of allowed luggage each. This was secured on the outside under tarps. Buffalo skins and sheepskins were given to riders if the weather was wet, windy or cold. A great horn such as those hanging from the rafters in the BA's lobby would announce the stagecoach nearing the stage stop. The innkeeper and stable hands would prepare to receive the guests, and the meal service would be readied. Crowds would gather to see the strangers and hear their stories. Mail and newspapers would be anxiously received and read. The noon meal, dinner, was the high meal of the day, and the food is often described as bountiful. The evening meal, supper, was far less of an occasion. Breakfast was early and similarly less substantial than dinner (but it often included such things as "beefsteaks," fish, cakes, eggs and breads). The additional fare for meals and lodging, usually one dollar per day, was paid directly to the landlord. (It was expensive to travel in these early days, so it was not for everyone. The average wage in the early 1800s for someone not working on a farm was roughly one dollar a day.)

Opposite: Advertisements for stage service on the Post Road to Albany. Top left, clockwise: September 7, 1804 *(New York City) Evening Post*; March 14, 1815 *Albany Register*; November 28, 1815 *(New York City) Evening Post*; February 4, 1818 *(New York City) Mercantile Advertiser*. *Found in the collection of the American Antiquarian Society, used with permission.*

Often, stops were very quick in order to remain on schedule. Particularly punctual stages were known as "diligence stages." Passengers could also ride the regular mail stage or the "convenience" stage. The latter was on a less demanding schedule. Stages were also divided between main line and trunk line stages.

TRAVEL JOURNALS

By the early nineteenth century, travel journals through America were becoming especially popular in Europe. Not many journals exist for this area, but the few available in the public record serve to provide some insight into what it was like traveling through the Rhinebeck section of the Albany Post Road.

In 1786, a two-volume travel journal was published in Paris called *Travels of the Marquis of Chastellux in North America in the years 1780, 1781 and 1782*. Chastellux was a nobleman and general in the French army under Rochambeau and a sympathizer with the American cause. Hasbrouck's *History of Dutchess County* provides a synopsis of his local journey, paraphrased:

Having landed at Newport, Rhode Island, in July 1780, he traveled through Connecticut to the military depot in Fishkill. He intended, when he arrived in Fishkill, to stay in the "tavern of Colonel Griffin," but it was full. He then went to a "mediocre" tavern kept by "an old Madam Egremont." He tells us, "The house had not the cleanliness that one commonly finds in America; but the greatest inconvenience was that several panes of glass were lacking." Two years afterward, he passed through Fishkill again and stayed at the same tavern, but he found it was owned by "Mr. Boero'm" and the "house changed to its advantage, and had a very good dinner."

From here, he visited West Point and then Philadelphia. On returning in December 1780, he stopped in Newburgh and was entertained overnight by General Washington. He was then escorted by Washington himself on his barge to Fishkill Landing "to take the road on the east which travelers prefer to that on the west." From here, he headed north to see the battlefield at Saratoga. He could not find an Inn in "Pokepsie" because Governor Clinton and the Court of Sessions were meeting. He traveled three miles north of the city to "Prides Tavern." (On the east side of the road, south of West Dorsey Lane near a small creek, there was a tavern here in 1810 called Gay's Tavern. It is possible Pride's was on this spot, which is roughly three miles north of the city.) After an overnight, he left on a stormy winter day and proceeded through Staatsburg, where he was invited to warm up and dine with a curious and generous resident. He declined, pushing onward to Rhinebeck. He tells of his visit:

> *At Rhynbeck, no one leaves his house to ask me to dinner, but the snow mixed with hail was so cold, and I was so fatigued keeping up my horse upon the ice; that I should have stopped at that place even if I had not been invited by the good appearance of the Inn, called "Thomas' Inn." Although it was only half past two o'clock, seeing that I had so far made twenty-three miles, that the house was good, the fire well lighted and the proprietor a big man of good mien, a hunter, a horse merchant and disposed to talk, I decided, according to the English expression, to "dispense with" the rest of my journey...After we had talked commerce, we talked agriculture. He told me that all the land about Rhynbeck was of extreme fertility... The 23rd (December, 1780,) I left the Thomas Inn at eight o'clock in the morning and travelled for three hours, always in the district of Livingston (Livingston Manor). The road is beautiful and the country rich and well cultivated. You go through many quite considerable hamlets. The houses are fine and commodious, and everything there announces prosperity. In leaving that district you enter into that of Claverack, where you descend the mountains and approach the Hudson River.*

This Thomas' Inn is in Upper Red Hook off Spring Lake Road (once part of the Post Road). Red Hook was part of Rhinebeck until 1812. It still exists as a private residence and a historical marker outside notes it as the place General Putnam used for his headquarters briefly in 1777. Colles's atlas places it right next to milestone 106 (which no longer exists).

Another brief journal entry, or letter, in this case, is found in P. Smith's 1887 *General History of Dutchess County*. He cites a letter from "Mrs. [Margaret] Livingston to the Judge [Robert], her husband," giving the details of a journey from New York City to Clermont (she possibly stayed in her old home where her father still lived):

> *Clermont, July 12th, 1766*
> *...We had a very pleasant ride the first day (from New York) which brought us to Croton. Here we were detained until the next day by rain, but it is impossible to describe this next day's journey; the crags, precipices and mountains that we had a view of, together with the excessive badness of the roads, that were laid bare by streams of water taking their course through*

the midst, which made it very disagreeable to me. We could go no further that day than Warren's, who lives in the midst of the Highlands, but the next day made up for the fatigue of this. We had a most charming journey the remainder of the way. We breakfasted at Van Wyck's who lives at Fishkill; dined at Poughkeepsie, slept at Rhinebeck, where we arrived at six o'clock.

In 1794–95, the English diplomat William Strickland traveled through the area. His journal is in the possession of the New York Historical Society.[62] On October 9, he traveled from Fishkill north. Somewhere near Hyde Park, "before Judge Lewis' house a little farther up the road," he mentions a tavern owned by "Jackson," which has a commanding view of the "Kaastskill" Mountains. He reached Rhinebeck that evening and tells us:

In the evening we arrived at a Tavern at Rinbeck-flats kept by one Potter. Here without asking for any thing particular we orderd refreshments and at seven o'Clock sat down to our meal, the last taken in the day consisting of tea and coffee, beef steaks and cheese, bread and butter and cakes of various kinds, milk and eggs, sweetmeat and peaches, Rum and Madeira; dinner this may be called, or tea, or supper or what you please, travellers usually take two meals a day, and the Innkeepers make little difference what they provide, whether it be the first or the last; however with such variety and plenty we had every reason to be satisfied, and if such continue to be provided, and we are told we shall generally meet with such, there is no reason to complain of the hardships attending travelling in this country. Another pleasant circumstance also attends it: there is no craving waiters and hostlers expecting their fee and dissatisfied when they have got it; the servants of the house do what is wanted, as it is for their master's interest; the master usually brings in his bill, receives his money, and gives the accurate change, if change was necessary; where anything to be offered to him, he would be offended; he has done you no favour, you have done him none; he has accommodated you, you have repaid him; the obligation is mutual, and evenly balanced; therefore he receives your money without thanks; he treats you with civility, if you treat him so, and feels that you are perfectly independent of each other; at first there is some little difficulty for an Englishman to adopt similar sentiments; but when familiarised to them, he reaps the benefit of them by finding the innkeeper here, a superior character in intelligence and respectability, to what he has been accustomed to in his own country.

The day has been remarkably pleasant for travelling; the sun warm at noon; the morning and evening most genial. Wind S: W: and gentle.

To Poughkeepsie 16 miles, to Rinbeck-flats, 19.
Expenses of this day 29/9

The Potter that he mentions is Asa Potter, and Asa did not own the BA until 1802. Strickland traveled through roughly eight years earlier. According to the Thompson maps, a Potter Inn existed in town just north of the BA, near Platt Avenue.[63] Strickland must have stopped there, or there is a remote possibility Potter was running the BA at the time simply as the landlord and not as the owner. Bogardus, the aging owner, seemed like he had his hands full with his merchant and trading operations, so he might have "leased" out space to capture a piece of the developing stage business. This is just conjecture, and no records offer any support to this possibility.

Finally, James Stuart, traveling with his family in 1829, published his account in *Three Years in North America*.[64] Through Dutchess County, he tells us:

The passage through the Fishkill mountains is one of the most interesting parts of the Hudson; and the heights in the neighbourhood of Fishkill present the most varying and romantic views of the river, sometimes appearing in detached lakes, and from other points as a large sheet of water covered with numerous boats and shipping. The town of Newburg, and the villages and high grounds on the opposite side of the river, enliven the prospect.

The country from Fishkill to Poughkeepsie abounds with fine farms, which, I was told, might be worth about forty dollars an acre wherever the buildings attached to the land are tolerably good. To those who would purchase land already cleared, with a view to profit, I would rather recommend the banks of the Hudson, within from thirty to fifty miles of New York, where the farmers have succeeded in establishing steamboats, in order to carry their produce daily to that city.

Poughkeepsie is the capital of Duchess County, and a considerable place. Swift's Hotel, where we dined, is as handsomely furnished as any country hotel I have seen anywhere...The drive from Poughkeepsie to Hyde Park and to Rhinebeck passes through a rich undulating country, the ground on the banks of the river commanding as pleasing views as can be imagined. There is a greater number of country seats than I have seen anywhere away from the great towns upon this line of country. They belong to Mr. Broome, Mr. Holebrooke, Dr. Allen, Mr. Macrae, Dr. Hosack, Mr. Wilks, Judge

Pendleton, and Messrs Livingstone, originally from Scotland, who have a great territory here…Dr. Hosack's terrace is the finest that I have seen on the river, and possesses views, ending with the Catskill mountains in the distance, that can hardly be surpassed. A great number of workmen are at present employed by him in extensive improvements upon the grounds, and the enlargement of his mansion-house.

This is the Vanderbilt National Historic Site, along with land on the east side of the Post Road. Before Hosack bought it in 1828, it was the estate of three generations of the Dr. John Bard family. Stuart continues:

The evening was cold when we arrived at Jacob's Hotel, at Rhinebeck, and we therefore ordered a fire. They brought us, as usual, very good coffee, homemade bread, some hot meat, butter, preserves, &c. We had concluded our repast, when the waiter came in and laid the cloth for one person, in the corner of the room, and set upon it a new edition of the very same articles which we had had, for our driver. I presume this was done on account of the room being rendered more comfortable by the fire we were enjoying. The driver is a very modest person, and made his exit as soon as he had finished his meal. We have not hitherto, during the whole of our journey, seen anything like a poor man's house, or a beggar, or anyone who did not seem to be well-clothed and fed. As few people are walking on the public road as in other parts of this country: all are on horseback, or in their dearborns, or other carriages. One of the greatest annoyances in travelling here arises from the bed-rooms being almost universally meagerly furnished. A bed, without curtains, even where requisite, and with far too narrow bed-clothes, a couple of chairs, with a basin-stand, a small table, and a small looking-glass, form the sum total of what is thought necessary for a bed-room. A sufficient number of basins and of other things is hardly ever provided, unless they be particularly desired. Though this house is small, there is a considerable library in it, chiefly relating to religion, to law, and to grammar. The waiters at all the houses where we have been, excepting at Fishkill and Poughkeepsie, were females, white women, and uniformly obliging, although they would not have accepted a shilling had it been offered; but at Fishkill, there was a little boy of colour, who, as usual, was looking out for his fee. Both Rhinebeck and Poughkeepsie, originally peopled by the Dutch, still resemble very much Dutch towns. Rhinebeck is upon a fine plain, at a considerable height above the Hudson, from which it is about two miles distant.

We left Rhinebeck early in the morning, with the thermometer at 45°, and went on to a small hotel about a mile beyond Redhook, about eleven miles, to breakfast, for which we were quite ready when we got there.

When referring to Rhinebeck, Stuart likely meant to say "Jacques Hotel," not Jacobs. The BA, by then the most prominent hotel in town, was operated by the Jacques family from 1805 to 1837, though, oddly enough, Jacob H. Tremper operated the BA from 1837 to 1840. Also coincidentally, the Thomas Tavern in Red Hook was owned by Jacob Thomas, but Stuart seems to have stopped elsewhere in Red Hook (he mentions his stop was at the house of Garret Cucks).

Unrelated to Post Road travel, there was one other curious account of a visit through Rhinebeck posted in the May 22, 1802 *New York Mercantile Advertiser* newspaper.[65] It seems that Election Day in Rhinebeck was not for everyone. A traveler by the name of Roger Buffaloe reported:

Sirs, Agreeable to your request I sit down to give you some account of my journey to the northern part of this state, the state of the country, the circumstances of the people, and the adventures arising out of 300 miles, partly by land, partly by water. I left New-York the 23rd of April, landed at Rhinebeck on the 25th. This is a part of Dutchess county, and very flourishing, because the land is generally very good. The election, which was just at hand occasioned some stir, much swearing and grog-drinking, and no little bad disposition between neighbours. The right of choosing our representatives, if a blessing, is here, as well as in other places, grossly abused, for the idleness it occasions and the bad habits it necessarily promotes, become a curse to many. I tarried here no longer than was absolutely necessary to do the business for which I was called, but proceeded over land to Albany, which I reached on the 27th.

CHANGING IMPORTANCE OF THE POST ROAD

During the 1840s–early 1850s, the stagecoach business was at its height of prosperity and glory—but this was also the beginning of its end. Robert Fulton's steamboat had been successfully demonstrated thirty-three years earlier (and an 1824 Supreme Court case had since broken up its monopoly), so by now steamboats were carrying the bulk of the freight and many of the

Matthias Wortz's livery stable at the west corner of West Market and Garden Streets, almost right across the street from the Beekman Arms. The image is undated, but Matthias sold his business in 1899. Note the stage carrier labeled "Hotel." Barely discernable over the windows is the word "Rhinebeck," so this was a stage likely dedicated to the BA. Later photos of the same building show the Wortz sign replaced by "Fraleigh Bros Livery, Exchange, Stage, and Stables." *Courtesy of the MRH.*

passengers on the long-distance trip up and down river.[66] Steamboats could make it to Albany in less than twelve hours. The Erie Canal's opening in 1825 also added to the riverway's importance. In 1844, the telegraph came, and then in 1848 came the railroads. Commodore Vanderbilt's New York & Harlem Railroad reached Poughkeepsie by 1849 and Rhinecliff by 1851.

Although ships and then rail displaced the long-haul stage, stagecoaches were still needed to move people and products from the landing to the main road and between other stops in town. They also remained an important part of travel to towns not directly served by rail. Rhinebeck continued its stage service from the station in Rhinecliff to the "old hotel" and to various other stage stops. These local stage lines existed until the arrival of the automobile. In 1902, the first "automobile stage" appeared between Rhinecliff and Rhinebeck, an enterprise financed by J.J. Astor, L.P. Morton and A.L. Wagner.[67] Calvin Rikert, a noted early stage operator, gave up his stage line to the Hub Garage in April 1914. The Fraleigh Brothers (F.J. and John) stage line was the last to exist in Rhinebeck, having taken over Matthias Wortz's

RHINEBECK LIVERY STABLE,

(near the Rhinebeck Hotel,)
H. GERMOND, Proprietor.

The subscriber has constantly at his Stables, and ready for service at a moment's notice, single or double teams, and vehicles of every style for the accommodation of customers. Horses let by the hour, day, &c. Ample accommodations and good stabling for travellers' teams.

Entire satisfaction is assured to the patrons o this establishment. Charges moderate.

H. GERMOND.

Sept. 12, 1859.   32:tf

Regular Mail Stage Line.

THE SUBSCRIBER continues to run carriages between Rhinebeck village and the Depot, attending all the Passenger Trains of the Hudson River Railroad, and conveying passengers to their residences in any part of the village.

Carriages in readiness to attend at funerals, when desired. While thankful for the liberal patronage hitherto received, the subscriber trusts by strict application to business, and his endeavors to accommodate the travelling public, to merit a continuance of popular favor.

JOHN TAPPING.

Rhinebeck, April 24th, 1860.

☞ Mr. John Tapping is Agent for the American Express Company for Rhinebeck and vicinity. Packages entrusted to him will be promptly forwarded to their destination.

Advertisements for stage service from the train station to the village in the *Rhinebeck Gazette.* Both ads had been running for a while. *Found in the newspaper collection of the RHS, used with permission.*

business in December 1899. It, too, converted to the horseless carriage in the early 1900s.

When the automobile became practical for the masses, the Post Road emerged again as an important travel route. People were no longer burdened by the limitations of the rail and felt a new freedom to explore. By the 1920s, the Post Road became the most commercially significant byway in the state. The country drive—a new leisure activity popularized by the American Automobile Association (AAA), Duncan Hines restaurant recommendations and local economic development articles—brought vehicle traffic to many scenic areas. Rhinebeck's Catskill views and its historic Beekman Arms made it a popular destination. By the late 1950s, with the expansion of IBM and development of several commercial strips, the road became a travel juggernaut from Poughkeepsie south. In September 1966, the Arterial Highway around Poughkeepsie, another Albany Post Road reroute, was opened to traffic.

CHAPTER 4

Traphagen's Early Settlement

Settlement began in the village area soon after the Post Road was forged through the wilderness. By now, early explorers and surveyors had already left their marks on this land. The full extent of the Landsman Kill would have been reconnoitered and nine waterfalls suitable for water power identified. By 1774, all would be turned to mill sites and utilized (Morse points out nineteen mills, though some were on the same site). Sawmills and gristmills were the earliest types, but later, woolen/carding, plaster, oil (flaxseed, linseed, rapeseed, etc.) and paper mills found commercial viability.[68] Beekman's mill at the falls in Vanderburgh Cove (on the Hudson) was thought to be one of the first in Dutchess County, circa 1710. In January 1719, William Traphagen sold back to Henry Beekman's son the six acres off the southeast angle of his property "for conveniancey to errect mills thereon" so the two mills in the village likely were built at some point after this date.[69]

The location of the community that became the Village of Rhinebeck seemed ideal. Here at the trail intersection with the new Queen's/King's Highway, a spring was located. Later, this was capped, and a common-use pump was installed circa 1765 (according to Morse, who states that it remained until 1895, though postcards still show it as late as 1910). The surrounding land was relatively flat and fertile once cleared of the trees and rocks. The natives were peaceful. Just down the hill was a waterfall with the perfect topography for a mill pond and two mills.

Reminiscing back to these early days, one can just imagine the weary traveler on his way to Albany, exhausted after twenty miles of travel from

The 1922 dedication ceremony of the DAR plaque marking the crossing of the King's Highway and Sepasco Indian Trail (Foster era). The plaque points out that over the trail "the Connecticut pioneers [traveled] to their new homes in western New York." A November 11, 1922 *Rhinebeck Gazette* article of the ceremony notes this area as being called "Beekman Square." *Courtesy of the RHS.*

his last rest, hearing the waterfall of the Landsman Kill, crossing the roughly hewn log bridge near the churning gristmill, approaching the nascent village on the rise and finding food and shelter at one of these early homes/taverns. The village was very small, perhaps containing the mill and just a few houses and farm lots. The necessities of the town—the blacksmith, the early meetinghouse, the doctor and the tavern/trading post—were all likely situated within these homes. As late as 1756, historian William Smith writes of Dutchess County: "The only villages in it are Poghkeepsing and the Fish-Kill though they scarce deserve the name."[70] Still, as late as 1779, when Erskine came through, only eighteen structures existed in the immediate village area, including the church and a gristmill. One extended family who did reside here and who populated a good part of the earliest settlement was the Traphagens.

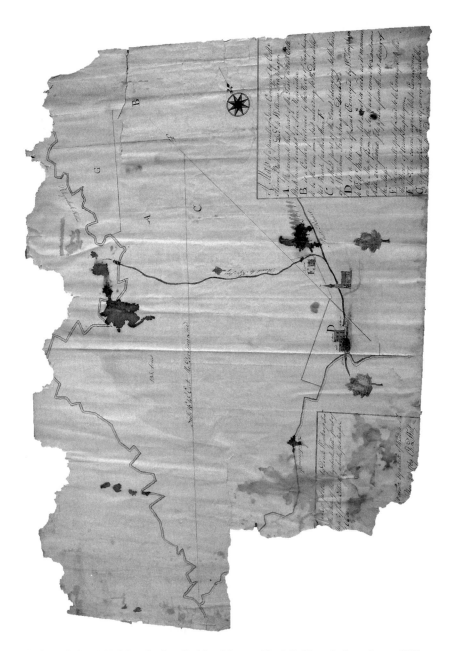

Full view of the 1769 *Map of a Parcell of Land Conveyed by Coll. Henry Beekman Dec. to William Traphagen*, showing the split of territory between William and Arie. Arie's land was sold back to Colonel Beekman by 1765. The legend points out a surveying mistake even back then, noting a failure to close a boundary around the mill. The triangle plot seems to take on a new shape from the 1746 original exchange, adding a few yards to the north, west and east. *Used with permission of the Princeton University Library.*

The Traphagen Family

With an eagerness to start development, Judge Henry Beekman (merchant) sold to William Traphagen (wheelwright) 281 acres of prime forest and farmland on May 25, 1705. As far as any records show, this transaction was Beekman's first from his patents. William and his heirs were to pay Judge Beekman and his heirs six schillings a year "forever." On the same day, William immediately split this property in half with his stepson Arie Hendricksen (son of Hendrick Ariaensen, William's wife's first husband) for a sum of one hundred pounds current money. Arie was given the western half, split from where the Landsman and Rhinebeck Kills join, extending north on a line that runs just behind the current Starr Library.

Arie received this property when he "came of age" through another deed dated February 17, 1710/11. He listed himself as a cooper (a barrel maker) and had a brewery on his property.[71] On June 4, 1706, Traphagen sold 24 acres to Jacob Kip (cooper) for nine pence a year.[72] On January 1, 1719, William purchased for 100 pounds another 290 acres south and east of the Landsman Kill from Beekman's son, and he also sold Beekman the mill property.[73] William was also involved in a number of other transactions and leases to other parties throughout his life.

William (1664–1738) was the second-oldest son of Dutch immigrant William Jansen Traphagen (or Trophage, 1642–1688), who settled in this country in Bushwick, Long Island, about 1660. By 1664, the elder William J. had moved to Kingston and began acquiring land. William J. married three times and, in doing so, spread the Traphagen lineage to some of the more famous early Dutch settlers in the region. The Traphagens are tied to the Burhans, Winnes, Ostranders, Piers and Kiersteds. In William J.'s will, dated February 16, 1685, he gave all of his property to his three sons and divided the rest of his estate among his three sons and two daughters.[74]

Rhinebeck's William, William J.'s son, married Tryntje Peele about 1695 in Ulster County. She died before 1699 in Kingston with no children. William then married Gepje Arentsen Pier, the widow of Hendrick Ariaensen (or Aryance), in Kingston on April 30, 1699.[75]

William must have been industrious and skilled. He was a wheelwright, a craftsman who makes wagon wheels and likely mill gears, and knew his way around the landscape of the trail intersection. His relationship with Judge Henry Beekman in Kingston is not described, but in such a small town, they surely knew each other. Their names show up together on the same 1711–13 Ulster County Town Supervisors Reports, Beekman always for compensation for travel and legal services, William to be paid as a messenger and in one case for a load of wood (others on this report are there to be compensated for killing wolves).[76] As mentioned, Morse tells the tale that Judge Beekman brought William over to Rhinebeck to build the mills, which very well could be true given all that was accomplished.

Though he acquired the land in 1705, census and tax records suggest William moved across the river to Rhinebeck sometime between 1715 and 1717. Recorded history unfortunately leaves us no epic tale of his life. All we really know of this pioneer comes from traces that he has left us in deeds, lists and in other official documents. He was still in Kingston when his youngest child was baptized in 1708.[77] By 1710, William might have been engaged in building his first Dutchess County mill in Vanderburgh Cove and was simply "commuting" over from Kingston. William Traphagen's name was not on the first census of Dutchess County, taken in 1714. The tax roll of January 17, 1717/18, is the first record of "Wellem Trophage" appearing in the County. (He's shown as the sixth wealthiest of the sixty-four men assessed in the North Ward of Dutchess County.) On August 26, 1730, William was listed with Lawrence Osterhout and Jacob Kip on a deed for two acres presented by Henry Beekman for the Reformed Dutch Church of Rhinebeck (RDC). William Traphagen also appears in the first *Book of the Supervisors* from 1718 to 1722 and is mentioned in Hasbrouck's *The History of Dutchess County, New York* as the first supervisor of the North Ward for 1720 and 1721 (to be replaced in 1722 by Hendricus Beekman). He was elected North Ward supervisor on April 7, 1724, and is listed at least through 1728–29 on the tax assessment record for the North Ward of Dutchess County.[78] By 1740, the W. Traphagen name no longer appears on the census.[79]

William made out his will on April 27, 1736. The 1738–39 tax record for Rhinebeck lists "the widow of William Traphagen," so he appears to have passed away sometime before 1739 (when he was roughly seventy-five years old).[80] Interestingly, a later property mortgage dated February 12, 1790, of the Traphagen land mentions "Lot #1" (discussed later) that contained a one-quarter acre "burying place." It is possible the family plot was here. There does not seem to exist any record of a Traphagen in the church or town cemetery, though Morse says they are buried in the RDC.

William and Gepje had four children. Their first child, Johannes, is believed to have died young. They had three other children.[81]

WILLIAM JR. (born 1703) was the oldest surviving son. He married Maria Dircksen on August 24, 1750. William was a deacon in the RDC in 1752. He is listed on the Slaveholders Census of Dutchess County on April 2,

When Howard Morse wrote his *History of Rhinebeck* book in 1908, he had his friend Edwin V. Marquardt fill it with illustrations. This one of the Beekman Arms has become somewhat iconic. A stained-glass reproduction of this sketch has hung behind the bar since at least 1941. Morse tells the reader the picture is circa 1789 and the place was built by Arent about 1766. This drawing and age claim, of course, are just speculation (and Arent appears to have died by 1747). The Dutch gambrel roof does not seem to appear on the 1797–98 map just a few years later. This 1908 picture looks somewhat similar to, and was perhaps influenced by, a sketch made in 1905 of the Fraunces' Tavern in New York City by the noted English engraver Samuel Hollyer.

1755, and he was a signatory of the Petition of Association in June 1775. An August 29, 1908 *Rhinebeck Gazette* article recollecting the memory of an old citizen identifies William Jr. as a mill owner in Rhinebeck, along with his brother-in-law Isaac Cole, father of Simon. This was likely the lower mill on the flatts. The old-timer adds, "The date of its erection was marked on a beam 1750 W. T.-I. K."[82] William is thought to have had no children.

GEESJE, their daughter, was baptized on April 15, 1705, in the Kingston Reformed Dutch Church and probably died at Rhinebeck. She married Isaac Cole (Kool) on October 3, 1731, in the RDC. Together, they had seven children: Willem (twin, baptized and presumed born 1732, possibly died young); Rebecca (twin, born 1732), married Benjamin Van Steenburg; Simon Isaac (born 1735), married Marietje Trompoor; Johannes (born 1737); Lena (born 1740), married Henry Shaw; Geesje (born 1743), married Johannes Van Fredenburg; and Sara (born 1747).

ARENT was baptized at the Kingston RDC on June 20, 1708, and died in Rhinebeck about 1747. He married Lea Van Etten in the RDC on September 14, 1739. Arent and Lea Traphagen had five children: Rebekka (born 1740) married Cornelius Radcliffe; Cattarina (born 1741) died young;

Lea (or Leah, born 1743) did not marry, but she shows up as a witness to the baptism of one of Everardus Bogardus's children; Willem (born 1745) probably died young, as there are no records for him; and Catharina (born 1746) married Peter Radcliffe.

On June 25, 1741, Arent and William Jr. distributed the property specified in their father's April 27, 1736 will to their sister.[83] Arent was still alive on August 26, 1746, when he exchanged the triangle property mentioned earlier with Henry Beekman. He likely passed away between December 4, 1746, when he is listed at his daughter Catharina's baptism in the German Reformed Church, and February 5, 1747, when his widow appears on the next tax list.[84] Arent equally distributed his estate amongst all his children. None of the daughters appear to have taken over Arent's estate after he died, as their cousin Simon Cole seems to have been in possession of at least some of it. Simon possibly became the heir through the rights of primogeniture, if recognized. In England and Holland, this would have the firstborn male child inheriting the entire estate to preserve the family wealth and heredity. Simon seemed to be the oldest surviving "collateral" male, being a nephew.[85]

CHAPTER 5

Origins of the Beekman Arms

A rent Traphagen's 1746 triangle land exchange tells how and when the land around the BA was secured. Twenty-three years then pass before any evidence of the actual building surfaces. The few facts that do appear

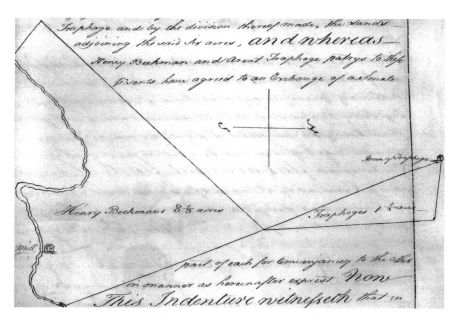

August 26, 1746 land indenture between Colonel Beekman and Arent Traphagen, each heirs to their fathers' estates. "House of Traphage" appears to the right (the BA would be below it). This is a copy of the original deed preserved in the DCRD Ancient Documents Book, also Book 5, p.399, and also filed as map# 2416.

between 1769 and 1779 are useful but incomplete. Nothing provides the "why" or "how" the BA actually came into existence. Since Smith and Morse appear to have been hindered by the same lack of supporting evidence, the records seem long lost.[86] Fortunately, several old deeds and maps do exist to help describe the earliest settlement.[87] Knowing how the settlement developed helps get us closer to that time period, and it provides insight into the possible origins of the BA.

THE EARLY VILLAGE SETTLEMENT

In the 1741 distribution of William Traphagen's estate, both Arent and William Jr. identify themselves as "yeoman," which in the eighteenth and nineteenth centuries was a non-slaveholding, small landowning, family farmer. Notably, neither calls himself an innkeeper or merchant. Geesje's husband, Isaac, also notes himself as a yeoman on the 1769 sale of their property, so all three of William Traphagen's children were farmers for at least part, and presumably all, of their lives. Being farmers, their properties were relatively spread out. From the old deeds, descriptions of their lots surface as "Geesje Home Lot" (twenty-two acres, technically "*Twenty Two Acres, Three Roods, and Sixteen Perches*"), "Arent's Home Lot" (fifteen acres), Arent's one-and-a-half-acre triangle lot (on which the BA was built), "Lot #1" (forty-three-acre field owned by Arent), "Lot #2" (thirty-five-acre field owned by Geesje), a two-acre undivided woodlot and five-acre meadow lot. These lots covered a sizable amount of the future village area. William Jr.'s property is not specifically designated, but it was here as well.

MAPPING THE PAST

It would seem simple enough to take data from these eighteenth-century documents (reference points, angles, distances, boundary descriptions) and just re-plot the information on twenty-first-century maps to see where the lots were located. It turned out not to be that straightforward. Maps and deed surveys in the old days were based on measurements obtained using the tools and techniques of the day. Errors were clearly made. Furthermore, there were nuances in the old descriptions and maps. References to then-meaningful contemporary landmarks such as marked trees, rock piles, sides of roads, "lands owned by….", initialed stones and other unique locations ("beginning at a certain Krambery or poghkeeme fly") were often found. Most of these no longer exist, so it made finding exact locations very difficult.

Another problem, already alluded to, is that many important surveys, revisions and agreements were simply lost over time. It was not uncommon to record official documents with the county years after they were agreed to by parties. The 1746 triangle land exchange, for example, was not recorded until August 28, 1770 (likely when this property was to be transacted again). Arent's home lot description, another example, does not show up in the public record until 1790, roughly fifty years after it was first defined (it is mentioned to exist in 1741). There was effort and cost involved in traveling, getting witnesses and communicating with the registrar. The primitive state of early record management also did not help matters. Colonel Beekman had his own chest with his copies of the deeds and plot plans. Some deeds were water-stained and damaged; still others were noted as "not recorded."[88]

A few useful clues come from our old deeds and maps to help bring order to the investigation. The 1746 triangle plot roughly pins down the location of Arent's triangle and the mill lot. To go beyond that, one needs to work backward from 1802. After the Traphagen era, a merchant by the name of Everardus Bogardus purchased Arent's land, as well as other properties in the village. When he passed away some thirty years later, his son decided to sell the property, and the son must have had it resurveyed in 1802.

The plot starts at one of those long-lost markers, "a stone set in the ground marked HB (Henry Beekman)," so pinning down where this was precisely on the landscape required some deduction. The best modern-era map to use to find out where this lies on the landscape is the Dutchess County Parcel Access System tax map showing the current-day property outlines. Old borders sometimes transferred through the ages in the form of stone walls, geological features, confluent points or very old street layouts bound down by old houses that did not move.

For our map, keeping all of the distances, angles and shared borders of the 1802 deed intact, the plot simply had to be rotated slightly into place to best fit the complete outline. Laying out the 1802 Bogardus outline on the parcel map shows that the northern extension covers Oak Street, the right or easternmost part is Arent's triangle where the BA is located and the large block near the bottom is a field south of the Starr Library. This 1802 result provides a useful starting template.[89]

Likely locations of the original Traphagen family lots. This map combines somewhat isolated data from 1741, 1746, 1769, 1770, 1790, and 1802. Lot#1 and the BA/triangle lot seem placed near where they should be. Unrecorded changes (and recording mistakes) were clearly made. Dutchess County Parcel Map used in background.

Now layering in the old lots, the map starts to tell a story. The 1802 outline helps to reasonably place the location of Lot #1 and the extended 1746 triangle lot (several slight changes occurred through the years). Geesje's home lot abuts Lot #1, and two of its dimensions, as well as its acreage, are known, so this, too, was plotted. Geesje's far northeastern corner and Arent's lot share a cornerstone, and Arent's lot abuts Geesje's lot (and Lot#1) on the east. (It also runs along the Landsman Kill for a short distance.) Arent's home lot is briefly mentioned in 1741 and 1774, but the full description does not show up until 1790 when a mortgage for Bogardus describes it some fifty years after the first mention. Changes and resurveys clearly impacted this lot, as the boundary described is untenable.[90] The location drawn is where his lot was, but the boundaries are inexact.

A few notes of explanation might be useful to the reader:

1. The eastern border of the mill lot, the western border of the triangle lot and the backside of the Oak Street lots all line up somewhat close to the twenty-one-degree, forty-five-minute line. Everything east was Beekman's. This land was sold/leased over the years or donated to the church.

2. The top of the mill lot touches the 1746 triangle lot at a "stone set on the west side of the Kings High Road." South Street was a small dirt path (the path existed at least as early as 1744), so the intersection was a discernable landmark at that time.

3. The eastern corner of the mill lot is supposed to be a marked tree on the milldam, but 268 years later, the tree is long gone. Just like the 1769 map, the outline does not seem to exactly fit. The Post Road is seen coming from the south. The 1769 map shows it crossing the kill slightly west of where it crosses today. (Today, it crosses the kill over the Astor Bridge, donated to the town in 1911 by John Astor.)

4. The northwestern corner of the triangle lot was originally described as being at a "stone set on the south side of the road to Kip's Landing on the Hudson River." It seems to have moved by 1769.

5. Arent's estate included his home lot, Lot #1, the triangle lot and likely the property surrounding Oak Street. All this came into the possession of Everardus Bogardus likely by 1770.

6. The 1705 split of Traphagen's original grant to his stepson is a line following the tree line behind the new Starr Library.

7. The land north of Geesje's home lot and south of the back side of the Oak Street lot belonged to Hans Kiersted. It is described in a 1774 land exchange deed.

8. To be described later are the three houses marked: 1) what is believed to be Arent's house; 2) a second old stone dwelling house; and 3) the later homestead of Dr. Hans Kiersted.

THE STONE DWELLINGS AND ARENT'S HOUSE

Morse claims the original "Traphagen Tavern" was an old stone building belonging to William, now gone, that was located across West Market Street from the BA between Oak and Garden Streets (house #1). He tells readers the fanciful story that Arent, upon concluding that his father's "Traphagen Tavern" was too small and not well located, decided to erect his own tavern (the BA) closer to the intersection "before 1767." This may have been the oral history at the time, or Morse may have simply been giving his best possible explanation. No evidence exists to show this is factual.

This stone house on the north side of West Market Street was very old. It was still standing in the days of Morse and Smith, so they surely saw it and perhaps heard the oral history attached to it. It does have a Traphagen connection. An old 3/31/1868 *Rhinebeck Gazette* article predating both their books picks up on this dwelling: "'THE OLD STATE PRISON'—the old stone building in West Market Street, one of the first dwellings erected in this village and for years known as the 'Old State Prison,' has been purchased by William Pink, and is to be demolished. If the old house could talk it would undoubtedly tell of the gay old times held beneath its roof when 'egg-nog' and 'milk-punch' was around..."

Smith wrote thirteen years later in 1881: "This old dwelling house [being cited in Geesje's land distribution mentioned later] was doubtless the old stone house in West Market Street, called the 'old state[s] prison.' This was also pretty certainly the residence of William Traphagen, when he joined Lawrence Osterhout and Jacob Kip in the request for the land of the Reformed Dutch Church, in 1730, and was thus one of the first substantial houses built in this town." Later, Smith mentions the "old state prison recently taken down," suggesting it was demolished just before his book was published. (Smith could be incorrect in his attribution of this as the "old dwelling house" and as William's house.)

Morse writes similarly and expands on this in 1908: "[W. Traphagen] built in 1709 a stone house which served as a tavern, and in later years was known as the 'old state prison.' Why, is a conundrum. This house was on the north side of the Sepasco trail or path to the river, now West Market Street, and between Garden and Oak streets, in the village; it was torn down about 1882." (Morse, too, could be incorrect, and he follows Smith. Not much further support has ever been found on the prison reference.)

The 1746 land exchange seems to show this house as the "House of Traphage" at the west (top) corner of the triangle plot. The Dutchess County Registry of Deeds has the original deed, and the Princeton University archive has Beekman's original copy, which says more specifically "House of A. Traphage."[91] A later 1790 mortgage to the next owner (Bogardus) describes the triangle property simply as "lying near the late dwelling house of Arent Traphagen."

The 1746 land exchange identifies this triangle corner (and presumably the house) as being on the "south side of the road which leads to Kips Landing on the Hudson River." The Supervisor's Records of Dutchess County (Special Session held in the North Ward on May 14, 1722) also seems to mention this house (or another stone house nearby):

> *The Jury Sumoned according to the act of Assembly have viewed the Roads Leads through the Land of William Trophagen: en Areyan Hendricks and Says thay find a Conveniant Way for a Road Beginning from the Generall Kings High way Westerly by the North side of William Trophagen house and so along the Road now used and marked along by the brew house and then Southerly by & through & along the Edge of the Cornfield of Areyan Hendricsk to the Road that the Comissiors have Layd Whare it Leads through the creek.*[92]

There does appear to be some movement of this road and/or the plot boundaries, as the 1769 map (and 1802 Bogardus plot) shows this corner, and presumably the house, on the <u>north</u> side of the road. The 1769 plot appears to be a resurvey (though its accuracy is questionable).

An 1810 survey (DCRD Map #50) done for M.B. Livingston for the sale of four and three-quarter acres directly in the center of town (the northwest corner of the main town intersection) shows the BA (Jacques Hotel) seemingly along with this old notable stone structure (on the north side of the road). Plotting it out by using the distances provided on the survey shows that it was on the site of the current law office in town at 37 West Market Street (which is between Garden and Oak Street).[93] The house is illustrated in what looks like livable condition with a roof and windows and a tree in its front yard, but that may be reading too much into the sketch.[94] The

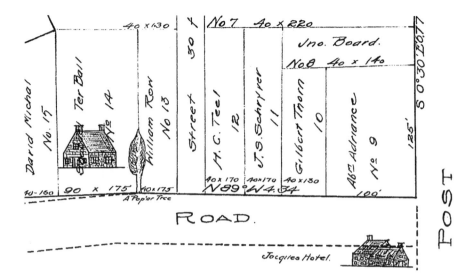

Excerpt from John Cox Jr.'s *A Map of 4 3/4 Acres of Land at Rhinebeck Flats Sold by M.B. Livingston to A. Adriance*. This map shows what may be the "old dwelling house" along with the BA. This 1920 copy is map #50 located in the DCRD. The 1810 original survey is said to no longer exist.

description of this lot in the actual deed document starts as: "Beginning at a poplar tree standing on the north side of the Turnpike road a little to the southeast of the kitchen and runs from thence..."[95] This is an oddly specific reference to find. Kitchens were often found outside and in back of homes. This does point to the likelihood that the road was once on the other side of this building. If this is the case, then the house and plot corner were once on the south side of the road to Kip's Landing as the 1746 deed noted. (Measurements from the dam also would seem to be off a little.) This house was possibly the dot in the fork drawn by Erskine. Once the south fork took over as the more dominant route, the north fork simply disappeared. This stone building seems to have become a store by at least 1796 (and probably sooner, by 1770).[96]

It is not clear if this house was ever occupied by William. Behind the BA, there is an old lane (two buildings west of the rear parking lot). This lane used to be the entrance to a second old stone house (house #2, in this vicinity) that was occupied by Dr. Hans Kiersted by 1766. Both the house and lane are cited in a 1774 land exchange between Everardus Bogardus and Kiersted. This later document simply mentions the old house was conveyed to Kiersted from the "heirs of William Traphagen (father to the aforesaid Aarant Traphagen)." This might be referring to Simon, as he appears to be an heir, and his name is the only one that appears in this era managing land transactions, or it might be referring to a collective group of heirs (including William Jr. Arent and Geesje). This house seems to be right on the border of Geesje's and Arent's properties. It seems very old, and it may have been William's.

The Second Old Stone House and Geesje

Geesje's home lot surfaces in the 1741 distribution of her share of their father's estate. This document gives Geesje four pieces of property: her home lot, Lot #2, a meadow lot and two acres of a nearby undivided wood lot. It goes on to describe her lot adjoining Arent's: "[Geesje's] home Lot begins by the North Easternmost Corner by a stone put in the ground which is also the Corner Stone of Arents home Lot." More interestingly, Geesje's home lot description mentions that it contains the "old dwelling house." The physical house and presumably the land underneath (as it was assigned in perpetuity) were divided in thirds, "out of which [Geesje's home lot] is Excepted and hereby is Reserved the Said William Traphagen and Arent Traphagen Their heirs and assignes forever two thirds of the old Dwelling house which Now stands on the said Lot."

Given the way the lots were plotted out, it seems likely the old dwelling was this second old stone house. "Old dwelling house" connotes both great age and possibly the historic family dwelling—both implying a connection to William. Even though it was on Geesje's lot (barely), and Geesje likely was allowed to live there, Arent and Williams did not want to give up rights to it, possibly because it belonged to the Traphagen (and not Cole/Cool) estate. (Though as fortunes would have it, Simon Cole seemed to ultimately become the heir twenty-eight years later.)

Geesje and Isaac sold their home lot and other property to their youngest son, Johannes, in 1763. (Interestingly, Simon is listed as one of the sellers and is specifically identified as "Heir at Law" on the document.) Johannes must have passed away, as the property was resold with an identically reading agreement on September 27, 1769, to Dr. Hans Kiersted.[97]

Dr. Kiersted actually seemed to have lived in this second stone house when he first came to town (in 1766, per Smith and tax lists). Smith tells us: "Dr. Hans Kierstead's first residence was the old stone house which stood

A few hundred yards just west of the main village intersection and the BA, the historic circa 1793 Kiersted/Heermance/Teller/Wells house still stands at 57 West Market Street. This house shows prominently on the 1798 Thompson map. *Courtesy of the RHS.*

on the south of the Wager lot, was taken down by Martin L. Marquet some years since, and reached by the lane referred to in the deed from Everardus Bogardus." He may have purchased it separately from Simon prior to buying the estate, or perhaps he was just renting. Twenty-four years later, Kiersted seems to have built a new larger house on his estate and moved across the street into house #3. Smith mentions: "A record in Martin Heermance's family Bible says: 'We moved into our new house, October 19, 1793.'" Heermance, marrying Sally Kiersted in 1789, was Dr. Kiersted's son-in-law. He went on to become a famous general and attorney. Presumably, Sally and Martin were living with Hans, and they all moved across the street together to this new house. Two of the Thompson maps show this house as Kiersted's, while the other two show it as Heermance's. It still stands today at 57 West Market Street. In addition to Geesje's home lot and the second stone house, Kiersted also seemed to have acquired the first stone house (Arent's) sometime around 1769. Simon Cole had it surveyed on March 27, 1770, and bought it back from Kiersted on July 3, 1770.

William Jr. appears to have been involved in the circa 1750 lower gristmill in town. Presumably, his home was somewhere near the mill complex. His father also owned a 290-acre parcel that was just south of the Landsman

Kill near the "Certaine Krambery or poghkeem fly or marsh where a certain tree stands marked on the south east angle of the land of Deirik De Duytzer."[98] Since William Jr.'s holdings do not show up in public documents, it is possible he inherited this acreage. Their father, William, also had all the land on the other side of Arent's, past Oak Street and running up to the Rhinebeck Kill (west of the twenty-one-degree, forty-five-minute line). This land also likely went to either William Jr. or Arent.[99]

THE BEEKMAN ARMS

Though Arent acquired the land the BA was built on in 1746, he does not seem to have been the builder. Arent identifies himself as a farmer, not innkeeper, and his hands likely were full farming and raising his five children. Arent did not live to an old age, passing away by 1747 at age thirty-nine, less than a year after he obtained the property. No evidence exists, other than Morse's tale, of Arent building the BA (and there is nothing in his will mentioning it).

Why he obtained the triangle lot next to his house can only be theorized. There did not seem to be a clear title issue, though perhaps in the day they thought there was one. The fact that Arent received only 1½ acres for the 2⅓ acres that Beekman received suggests Beekman had a little leverage in this exchange (if the land was valued the same). It is not clear why Beekman would need another 2⅓ acres around the mill or where exactly this 2⅓-acre parcel was situated.[100] It is possible there was a land dispute around Beekman's exact boundaries, and the triangle was a way to settle with Arent and compensate him. Arent could also have wanted the triangle lot because he was already farming this land or perhaps because he wanted clear access to the water supply at the spring. He may also have wanted the land to keep some road frontage property as the road shifted and moved.

Although all the signs point to someone other than Arent starting to build a structure here, there is still a chance he had indeed recognized the commercial potential of the corner, and as Morse claims, he built, or at least dreamed of or even started to build, a tavern or a house here. These were hardy people quite capable of anything.

On the 1769 map of the Traphagen property, the very first image of the building to become the Beekman Arms appears. Here, a two-story structure near the main intersection is noted as S. Coles.[101] We can only presume Simon

An enlargement of the earliest known drawing of the Beekman Arms, circa 1769. *Courtesy of the Princeton University Library.*

was involved in its appearance here. He was only eleven in 1746 when the property was first acquired, so any influence would have come later.

Simon was a merchant and not an innkeeper or farmer (at least not early in his life). He probably wanted a store here at the crossroad. He seemed reasonably wealthy, with land and possibly interest in a mill, so he might have had the financial wherewithal to have the building constructed.[102] Presumably, once the next owner came along and made him an offer (to buy or lease the new building), Simon chose a smaller building across the street to occupy.

The early BA, which was just the center part of the current structure (no south wing, north wing or third floor), was a fairly substantial two-story cut stone structure; it must have taken some effort and time to obtain the building materials and to construct it. It was not noted on the 1746 plot plan. A 1753 plot plan for the church lots across the street shows nothing on the west side of the road.[103]Although omission on these two documents is

The oldest photograph known to exist of the Beekman Arms (then the Rhinebeck Hotel). Note that at this time, the third floor did not exist. Taken from Halleck Welle's 1907 pamphlet *Reminiscences of the Oldest Hotel in America*. The date given was 1812, but early daguerreotype photography was not invented until 1838. Welles adds elsewhere in his text: "The alteration of the third story in 1865 did not materially change the interior below." This picture was also used in a July 14, 1907 Elmira, New York *Morning Telegram* article on the recollections of Sutherland DeWitt, a respected railroad man, with the following caption: "The Rhinebeck Hotel in 1812. The old Hotel showed no alteration from the above when as a boy I knew it in 1840–45."

not definitive, they just do not help any. Since it looks finished and complete on the 1769 map and it was here in 1779 per Erskine, the BA really could have been built anytime between roughly 1747 and 1769. The Coles and Traphagens were apparently busy building a mill in 1750, so that may have pushed the construction date of a new structure out a few years. The date that hangs over the door, 1766, is a best estimate, and it relies on Morse's comment that it was completed "before 1767." The torn 1769 note on the Princeton map, illegible today, may have been legible in Morse's day and perhaps was relied on for this comment.

One other theory exists on the BA's development. Arent's widow, Lea Traphagen, remained on the tax list through June 1748 and remarried Jacobus J. Kipp on October 24, 1748. A Jacob Kipp (there were several) is listed as a tavern keeper on the Rhinebeck tax lists from February 1755 until February 1762. There is a remote possibility it was Jacobus Kipp who helped build the structure and who ran it, perhaps with Simon as the lessor of the property.[104] Lea and Jacobus had four children together, so they were rooted in the growing community. The historical record unfortunately offers no further evidence to consider on this possibility.

Either way, the house appears to be in Simon's possession by 1769. Records are lost on exactly how and when Simon transferred the property to the next holder, a Kingston merchant and cousin (and possibly grandson) of an innkeeper, Everardus Bogardus. Bogardus does appear to have documented possession of the home lot in 1774 and the BA lot by at least 1790. Simon's will is filed in the surrogate court records.[105] He seems to have settled down on a farm straddling the Saw Kill, a few miles north of town. (The Saw Kill runs through Red Hook and out to the Hudson River near Bard College.) He gave this farm by "birthright" to his oldest son.

CHAPTER 6

Bogardus and the
Revolutionary War Era

Everardus Bogardus and his wife Arientie (Hoochtieling) likely took control of the Arent Traphagen estate in 1770. The fact that the 1746 triangle lot was finally recorded in August 1770 (so it could be transacted again cleanly) and that Simon Cole bought Kiersted's recently acquired dwelling in July 1770 (a place Simon could reside in or operate as a store when he presumably moved out of the BA structure) lend support to this possibility.[106] Bogardus seems to have come to Rhinebeck from Kingston by at least June 1760, according to the tax lists.[107] After acquiring the corner property and settling down next door to his friend Dr. Hans Kiersted, both realized they needed to do something with the property boundaries, as they were "not agreeable to the House Lots which the said parties have in possession, but interferes with each others improvements."[108] In 1774 they settled the matter. The agreement on record is the first one that ever mentions Bogardus as an owner of any of the Traphagen property. In this document, it cites Bogardus "owns by deed or conveyance" Arent Traphagen's "house lot" and a share of a woodland parcel.

Everardus (1738–1799) was of an Old Dutch family. He was the great-great-grandson of the "Dominie," the Reverend Everardus Bogardus of New Amsterdam, who was the second husband of the famous Dutch new world matriarch Anneke Jans. The Dominies' ten children would have children and grandchildren, and the family name would spread up and down the Hudson Valley, with many descendants settling in Albany and Kingston.[109] Interestingly, Anneke's will dated 1663 shows that one daughter married a

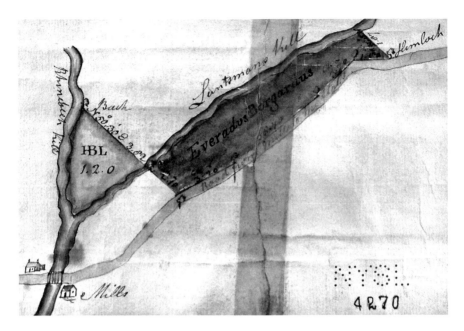

Illustration from the January 1, 1787 deed between Colonel Henry B. Livingston and Everadus Bogardus (merchant) for a two-acre lot located just south of the village on Mill Street (where the creeks meet). The lot is the large shaded area marked with Bogardus's name. *Courtesy of the New York State Archives, Henry Livingston Collection, SC19687 Box 2, Folder 2.*

Hans Kierstede. This Hans was very likely a forefather of the Rhinebeck Hans, so not surprisingly in this small world, the Bogardus and Kiersted families were tied together. Everardus's Uncle Everardus and/or his cousin Everardus Jr. were sloop captains, doing business with Beekman and possibly even with our Everardus.

On every deed and official document, Everardus listed himself as a "merchant" and notably not as a tavern keeper.[110] He seemed to be a businessman and land investor. Much of his acquired land was fertile farmland, so it is quite possible these were fields he used to grow wholesale produce for sale. His estate reached in parts all the way to the river and south to Staatsburg. He lived here in Rhinebeck in the BA structure with his wife, Arientie, and their nine children. Morse points out that both Bogardus and Kiersted each owned seven slaves, which is quite possible given all the land each had to manage (slavery in New York was not abolished until 1827).

The Bogarduses' tenure was in the middle of a defining era for our young country. Tensions between England and the colonies were rising. Word of the Stamp Act (1765), Townsend Duties (1767), Boston Massacre (1770) and tea parties in Boston (1773) and New York City (1774) agitated the population. After the battle at Concord and Lexington on April 19, 1775, citizens of New York were asked to sign the "Articles of Association," a pledge to determine who was dedicated to the cause of liberty. Rhinebeck was split, with 229 men—notably, Colonel Henry Beekman, Everardus and Benjamin Bogardus, Hans "Kierstead,"and Simon Cole—identifying themselves as Patriots and placing themselves under the power of the new government. The other 218 men of Rhinebeck refused to sign, either being loyal to the king or noncommittal (though it seems too important of an issue not to take a side).[111] The year 1775 was also when the great war hero, and one of Rhinebeck's most famous residents, General Richard Montgomery started his fateful trek to conquer Canada. He died in battle there on 12/31/1775.[112] Here in the colonies, the battle front shifted from Boston to New York in July 1776, bringing the region in closer proximity to the enemy forces. Locally, from 1776 to 1778 the critically important Fishkill Supply Depot was in operation near the intersection of the Post Road and the main road to Connecticut, now Route 52 (the depot stretched down to the Route 84 area). General Washington was briefly in residence there.

In October 1777, the Battle of Saratoga occurred just north of Albany. Fishkill's supplies were used to support the troops, as were Rhinebeck's mills. The Hudson carried most of the freight and arms, but large masses of armies and armaments were on the move up and down both sides of the river. After the battle, Rhinebeck's Reformed Dutch Church was used to house up to three hundred prisoners.[113] Some tried to escape and were shot. Militia troops were billeted in homes on the flats, and the area was extremely agitated. Nine days after the second Saratoga battle and running late for a planned rendezvous with General Burgoyne, a British expeditionary force sailed up the Hudson and set Kingston and the Livingston estate, Clermont, ablaze. Militia officer Barent Van Wagenen sounded the alarm in the countryside, possibly much like it had been done in the countryside of Middlesex County, Massachusetts, by Paul Revere.[114]

While Everardus appears to have stayed in Rhinebeck during this time (he is not on any enlisted or officer list in the county histories),[115]his brother Lieutenant Benjamin Bogardus of Kingston, New York, fought in the various battles around New York City and perhaps elsewhere. A short series of letters between Benjamin and Everardus were published in the March 14, 1925 *Rhinebeck Gazette*.[116] They briefly tell of the battle coming toward Benjamin in Westchester and the despair of the local inhabitants. In Dutchess County, Henry Beekman Livingston, Colonel Henry Beekman's grandson,

The 1939 post office next door to the BA with the NYS "Bogardus Land" historical marker in front. Technically the sign, designating this as William Traphagen's property, is incorrect. This was part of the triangle lot Arent, not William, acquired from Colonel Beekman. The small round window on the north side is meant to replicate where a cannonball supposedly struck the original house in 1777.

was placed in charge of the Fourth New York Regiment (Jacob Thomas, of Thomas' Inn, seems to have served at one point as a lieutenant). Hasbrouck tells us that four regiments were authorized by the provincial authorities in 1775. They were the First New York, Second Albany, Third Ulster and the Fourth New York Regiment from Dutchess County. Together, they were known as the Continental Line. Captain Henry Beekman Livingston and the Fourth New York Regiment were brigaded under General Montgomery. Under him, they marched to Canada and attacked Montreal and Quebec. They went on to fight at New York, Saratoga, Philadelphia-Monmouth and against the Iroquois in 1779. Local lore and a historical marker claim the land around the Beekman Arms was a "Training Ground of Revolutionary Troops." This very well could have been true, but nothing in the historical record speaks of it. More than likely, the Fourth New York was too busy

Rhinebeck's Dutch Arms Fife and Drum Corp "drilling" on the front lawn, likely around the bicentennial in 1975–76. *Courtesy of the Beekman Arms.*

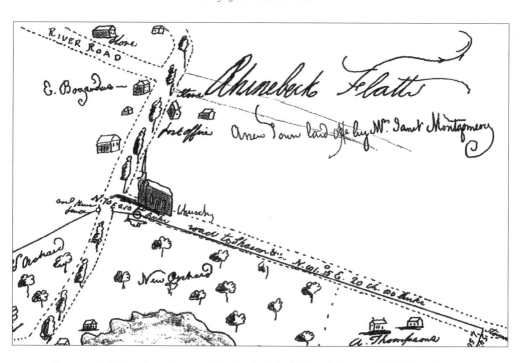

Excerpt of *A Map of an Allotment of Land on Rhinebeck Flatts, the Property of Col. Henry B. Livingston Containing about 44 Acres Land & Water* (just the tip of his land shows on this excerpt.) This September 30, 1796 map (copied in the 1920s) shows the BA as "E. Bogardus." DCRD map #2415. The county believes all the original maps no longer exist.

out in the battlefields, but home guards and local militia could have been practicing in the center of town. A designated central training ground was very common in this era.

During his tenure, Everardus amassed a sizable amount of real estate west, south and north of his property from various parties, including the Livingstons. In 1787, he bought land just south of the Landsman Kill from Henry Beekman Livingston. In 1789, Everardus exchanged two parcels of land he owned west of the village near the Rhinebeck Kill for three and a half acres with Dr. Hans Kiersted. There are other land transactions recorded, but these are unimportant to this story. In 1790, he took out a mortgage that appears to have been due in 1793. The record shows he was then "convicted" under a writ of *Fieri facias* for failure to pay his debts, and all his "goods and chattles" were confiscated from his estate a week after he died in 1799.[117]

WAS THE BA A TAVERN AT THIS TIME?

It was not a famous and notable tavern called "Bogardus' Tavern" of Revolutionary War days. Absolutely nothing in the record speaks to that. It was a residence, with possibly a mercantile/commodity trading business being operated from it. It may have had some space or a few rooms to let, but this did not seem to be its primary function. Two nearby stores were identified on a map in 1796 (one possibly being Cole's old store), and although Bogardus was a merchant, if his house was a retail store of any type, it likely would have been labeled similarly. Everardus's large landholdings suggest he had a significant supply of crops, livestock and minerals to sell, and being from a family of sloop operators, he may have been doing his business downriver. He also owned all the lots on both sides of Oak Street and probably had a fair amount of rental income coming in. His significant debts also lead one to believe he was an active businessman taking risks. A tally of the county court cases and claims Bogardus had against others for payment due shows sixteen such cases from 1767 to 1791.[118]

When the stage business started roughly in 1785, there is a possibility Everardus or a family member did adapt the building into a business/stage center. Its central location in town would seem a natural stop and transfer point to the river stage. Unfortunately, no evidence exists to provide any support of this activity. No early map marks the BA as anything but a significant house. On the 1798 Thompson maps (produced just before he passed away), the BA is not clearly noted as a tavern or inn like all the others on the map. It is seen more as a home owned by someone of prominence. Some hope that it was an old inn might be drawn from (only) one of the four Thompson maps, where the building seems colored like the other inns in town. Unfortunately, it is not labeled as an inn; rather, it is given the moniker "Montgomery Lodge," and the Bogardus name does not even appear. Another map says "Lodge Room," and it does include the name Bogardus next to it, but not much can be discerned from the map's faded color. The "lodge" may very well be referring to a masonic order that met here (Montgomery Lodge No. 66, organized January 8, 1798).[119] A lodge room would likely be in a non-official large town space, such as a hotel conference room or rental space in a business. It is strange, and perhaps telling, that these designations seem to have more importance to the mapmaker than noting it as a distinguished inn.

It could be argued that perhaps Bogardus's was just such a well-known inn that it did not need a special label. Unfortunately, nothing offers any support for that assertion. Both the fact that Bogardus does not list himself as an innkeeper (still a merchant as late as 1789) and that no early travel journals mention a tavern here cast further doubt. Years later, in the 1860s, the famous historian Benson Lossing came through Rhinebeck to research his book *The Hudson, From the Wilderness to the Sea*. He noted and wrote about all the old, historic buildings in town that mattered—and he completely missed the BA. This, too, points to the fact that in his era, the BA was just a fairly recent commonplace business. (Lossing lived locally in Poughkeepsie until 1838 and would have had a good sense of the hotel's status and importance.) Calling it the utilitarian "Rhinebeck Hotel" instead of something like "Ye Old King's Head" also did not help it secure an early historic reputation.

THE END OF AN ERA

The thirty years of Everardus Bogardus's presence in one of the most significant structures in town surely set a tone, and he must have been a notable force in town politics, religion and commerce. Change inevitably came. When he died at age sixty-one, he appears to have been in an illiquid position, having debts to pay but not being able to collect debts owed. His property was confiscated from him by the courts. None of his children seemed

At a Court held at the Surrogate's Office at Poughkeepfie, in the county of Dutchefs, the fourteenth day of May, in the year of our Lord one thoufand eight hundred—

PRESENT,

GILBERT LIVINGSTON, Surrogate of the county of Dutchefs.

WHEREAS Ariantje Bogardus, Philip Bogardus, and Benjamin Bogardus, adminiftrators of all and fingular the goods, chattels and credits which were of Everardus Bogardus, late of the town of Rhinebeck, in the county of Dutchefs, deceafed, by their petition prefented to the faid Surrogate, have fet forth—That the faid Everardus Bogardus was, at the time of his death, feized of real eftate in the county of Dutchefs, and not in any other county in the ftate of New-York, to the knowledge and belief of the faid petitioners.— That the petitioners have made a juft and true account of the perfonal eftate and debts of the faid Everardus Bogardus, as far as they have been able to difcover the fame, by which it appears that the perfonal eftate of the faid Everardus Bogardus, is infufficient to pay his debts, and therefore requefted the aid of this honourable court in the premifes, purfuant to the directions of the act, entitled, "An act concerning the Court of Probates," and the act therein referred to, entitled, "An act for the relief of creditors againft heirs, devifees, executors and adminiftrators, and for proving wills refpecting real eftates."

And Whereas, the faid petitioners have filed in the Office of the faid Surrogate, the inventory, and the accounts and eftimate in the faid petition mentioned, in due feafon, and under oath duly attefted.—Whereupon it is ordered, by the faid Surrogate, that all perfons interefted in the eftate of the faid Everardus Bogardus, do appear before the faid Surrogate at his office in the town of Poughkeepfie, county of Dutchefs, on the fourth day of July next, at two o'clock in the afternoon of that day, to fhew caufe, if any they have, why the whole of the real eftate, whereof the faid Everardus Bogardus died feized, fhould not be fold for the purpofe of paying his debts.   GILBERT LIVINGSTON.

May 24.   w raw 6w

Notice to anyone who has a claim against the Bogardus estate. Posted in the (New York) *Republican Watch-Tower* on May 28, 1800. *Courtesy of the American Antiquarian Society.*

to be in position to carry on his business. His eldest son, Benjamin, and wife, Maria, were living in Kingston at this time. His third son mentioned in records, Nicholas, died young, at age nineteen in 1794 (his small gravestone is right next to Everardus's very prominent one across the street behind the Reformed Dutch Church). The second eldest son, Wilhelmus, may also have died early. The other Bogardus children (born after 1776) may have been too young. It did not appear Benjamin was even interested in the business, as he collected debts owed, bought the property back and then negotiated a sale to the next owner, Asa Potter, as soon as he was able to clear the property through the courts.

CHAPTER 7

The Legends and Myths of Washington, Lafayette, Burr and Traphagen's Tavern

THE MYTH OF GEORGE WASHINGTON

There is an old legend that George Washington visited Rhinebeck and slept at the BA. As you might expect, it is very unlikely. The general's every move was recorded in diaries, expense books and copious correspondence. He appeared in southern Dutchess County down in Fredericksburg (now Pawling/Patterson, New York) and in Fishkill in October and November 1778, as winter quarters were being established at the Fishkill Depot. He wrote a letter to General Pulaski from Poughkeepsie on November 10, 1778. Beyond that, no record exists of him traveling any farther north in the county.[120] If he was milling about Rhinebeck, "looking out the windows of the old hotel," certainly he would have dispatched some letter or someone would have noted he was there. Further, it does not even appear the hotel was established yet, and Washington, when he traveled, generally received a warm reception with the area's wealthiest, most politically connected landowners. Staying at an inn/tavern was not out of the question, but Washington probably had his preferences.

The legend starts with Morse. He relays a third-hand story he heard about a farmhand who couldn't even remember if it was he or his father who saw Washington. Morse writes:

> *The redoubtable "Pete" Johnson used to tell of Gen. Washington visiting Dr. Tillotson at Linwood when he or his father was a boy*

working on the place. The time must have been about 1796. Here is Pete's story:

"Well, mebbe 'twasn't me, 'twas my ole dad who saw Gen. Washington. But he used to tell de story so plain dat any one hearin' him thought he'd been there hisself. The Gen'l, he rode on a white hoss, with green an' gold trimmin's. He wore a big yaller hat. He used to take off dat hat to a cullud pusson same as to a white pusson. Lawsy, 't made no difference to him. He was a real gen'leman, de Gen'l was. My ole dad, he run an' fetched a bucket o' water foh dat same w'itehoss. Yessir, he did, foh a fact. My ole dad was a boy at de time, an' de Gen'l he spoke toe him, true as Gospel. De Gen'l says toe him: 'Youse a bright boy. Go git him anudder bucket.' Yep, dat's w'at big Gen'l Washington says toe my ole daddy. Den de Gen'l got on his hoss an' went toe de ole Bogardus tavern on de flatts. He'd see Gen'l Armstrong and Gen'l Lewis and fab will 'em. He stayed ober night, an' de nex' mawnin' he was off agin foh New York."

If Morse's yarn is indeed true, quite likely the year is off, as Washington was not traveling in New York in 1796. Dr. Thomas Tillotson was a lieutenant in the Maryland Militia in 1776. In 1780, he was appointed by Congress to surgeon general of the Northern Department of the Continental army. He married Margaret Livingston, Margaret Beekman's daughter and sister of Chancellor Robert R. Livingston, in 1779 and settled in Rhinebeck after the war.

Local lore expands the story further by saying that Washington attended their wedding and danced with Margaret's sister Catherine. There is no record in Washington's papers of a visit at any time and very little mention at all by Washington of Dr. Tillotson.[121] However, with Washington being the socially aware person that he was, there is a remote chance he visited and the record was simply lost or nothing was ever recorded (he was in the lower Hudson Valley in 1779). Linwood is an estate near the Hudson River by Vanderburgh Cove and is quite accessible by sloop (though the wedding was on February 22, 1779, and the river was probably iced over, and Linwood was not built until circa 1794).

The misunderstanding may also come from another source. Washington indeed was at "Bogardus' Tavern"—but this was the more well-known Bogardus Tavern in Kingston. Marius Schoonmaker's 1888 *The History of Kingston, New York* contains the brief story:

On the 16th of November, 1782, Kingston was honored by a visit from General Washington, on his way, by a circuitous route from New Jersey

All that remains of Evert Bogardus's Tavern is this historic marker, at the corner of Fair Street and Maiden Lane (near the Old Senate House), Kingston.

to West Point. After passing the night of the 15ᵗʰ with his companion-in-arms Colonel Cornelius Wynkoop, at his homestead at Stone Ridge, which is still standing unaltered, and was for many years the residence of John Lounsbury, he proceeded on his way to Kingston…The arrival of the general and his suite was greeted with great rejoicings on the part of the citizens. He put up at the public house of Evert Bogardus, but accompanied by his staff, he dined with Judge Dirck Wynkoop, in Green Street. In the evening there was a gathering of ladies in the Bogardus ball-room, which was honored for a short time by the attendance of the general, when the ladies were severally introduced to him. The next morning at an early hour he left the village and continued his journey.[122] [It is possible Catherine Livingston danced with the general here.]

This Evert Bogardus (died 1810, son of Petrus) was the cousin of our Everardus (son of Nicholas) of Rhinebeck. Evert and Everardus were both grandsons of another Evert Bogardus (died 1717). On June 14, 1794, there was a public auction for Evert Bogardus's tavern in Kingston, as he, too, had debts he could not pay.[123]

THE MYTH OF LAFAYETTE

Contrary to the romantic views that the great French general Lafayette must have stopped in Rhinebeck and stayed at the BA, it is clear he did not. During Lafayette's U.S. visit from July 1824 to September 1825, every step of his trip was documented and published. He took a steamer ship called the *James Kent* up the Hudson and stopped at West Point, Newburgh, Poughkeepsie, Staatsburg (the mansion of Morgan Lewis, but only for an hour and a half) and, in this area, Clermont (just north of Rhinebeck) on September 16, 1824. Here he dined, reviewed troops, attended a ball and then returned to the ship. Earlier in the day, when the boat passed the Rhinebeck landing before reaching Clermont, Colonel Henry Beekman Livingston came aboard via a rowboat. Lafayette received him warmly. After Clermont, Lafayette briefly stopped at Catskill, Hudson and Greenbush the following day. From Greenbush, he took the ferry over to Albany. On Saturday, he visited Troy, and then he got back on the steamship and sailed straight through to New York City. Within days, he would start on his southern visit.

THE MYTH OF AARON BURR AND THE "PRE-DUEL"

Morse paints a colorful picture of Rhinebeck being the hotbed of political dispute in the region, with Aaron Burr's party taking residence at the local Rhinebeck tavern known as Tammany Hall and Morgan Lewis and his party (the Jeffersonian Republicans) headquartering at Potter's (the BA). Both sides were competing for the 1804 New York gubernatorial office. Morse wrote (over one hundred years later): "Very bitter feelings prevailed among the partisans of Burr and the Governor [Morgan]. It culminated in the duel between Burr and Alexander Hamilton, the brother in law of Schuyler."

The accessible historical record speaks of no great political match in Rhinebeck. Burr was only in town a handful of times, and nothing in his published memoirs makes any mention of the race.[124] An announcement found in the April 12, 1804 issue of the *Chronicle Express* (New York, found in the AAS) merely mentions that Burr was nominated for governor at the local party meetings in Rhinebeck and in the town of "Philips." There is no telling if he was even in these towns for the nominations.

Burr lost the gubernatorial race in April 1804, and this did not sit well with him. He blamed the loss partially on swing votes he did not get from Hamilton and partially on published insulting comments made against him by Hamilton and his faction.[125] He demanded an apology, which he did not receive to his satisfaction, and this was thought to be a significant contributing factor in the July 1804 duel.

There is another fanciful story about Burr and a duel at the Beekman Arms. Halleck Welles in his *Reminiscences of The Oldest Hotel in America 1700–1907* provides this one (he, too, wrote one hundred years after the fact, so there is no telling if this is factual):

> *The fireplace there is the same before which one night in 1813 Aaron Burr and Gen'l. John Armstrong sat chatting when Miss Eliza Jacques, daughter of the landlord, entered to pass through to the kitchen. Burr, who had just returned from the French court, imperiously ordered her to bring him a boot jack. She modestly replied: "It is not my place to bring you a boot-jack but I will order a negro to do it." Burr sprang up angrily and shaking his fist at her, shouted "By God! you are not too good to bring me a boot-jack!" General Armstrong sprang in front of Burr and shaking his fist in turn at him, cried: "By God, sir, she is too good to bring you a boot-jack and if you say that again I'll knock you down, sir!" Burr subsided; he knew the General was an expert swordsman.*

Confusing these two questionable incidents, the modern romanticized BA "fact" is that "it was inside the historic Hudson River Valley inn that rivals Aaron Burr and Alexander Hamilton exchanged insults that led to their infamous duel and Hamilton's death."

THE MYTH OF A TRAPHAGEN'S TAVERN

Historians can speculate, as we did in the opening, that being the first house in the region, Traphagen's house very likely was a natural wayside stopping point. Beyond that, there is no proof, and in fact, there is evidence to the contrary that a tavern ever existed here before the turn of the century. There is no map labeling any Traphagen structure as a tavern or inn; no newspaper accounts; no census, tax or innkeeper records; no later deeds that call a Traphagen anything but a "yeomen" (or wheelwright); and no written history.

Smith's 1881 history merely mentions that the Traphagens first owned the land the Rhinebeck Hotel was built on. Morse, in 1908, starts the Traphagen legend seemingly on his own. He provides undocumented material to support his story, such as a postrider advertisement.

This is a bit suspicious, as one of the very few archived advertisements for a postrider position was for one published in the *New York Northern Budget of Troy* on June 18, 1799.[126] Aaron Oliver informs the public of his service in this small ad.

Remarkably, Morse used this language almost word-for-word in the advertisement he created identifying the "Traphagen Tavern" on page 69 of his book: "The Post Rider wishes to inform the Publick that he is riding his Route regularly. All commands in his Line will be received with Thanks, and executed with Punctuality. Leave letters and Commands at Traphagen's Tavern. He returns his sincere Thanks to his former

NEWS! NEWS!

AARON OLIVER, *Poſt-Rider,*

WISHES to inform the Publick, that he has extended his Route; and that he now rides thro' the Towns of *Troy, Pittſtown, Hoofick, Mapletown,* Part of *Bennington,* and *Shaftſbury, Peterſburgh, Stephentown, Greenbuſh* and *Schodack.*

All Commands in his Line will be received with Thanks, and executed with Punctuality.

He returns his ſincere Thanks to his former Cuſtomers; and intends, by unabated Diligence, to merit a Continuance of their Favours.

O'er ruggid hills, and vallies wide,
He never yet has fail'd to trudge it;
As ſteady as the flowing tide,
He hands about the NORTHERN BUDGET.
June 18, 1799.

June 12, 1799 advertisement in the *Northern Budget* for a post rider. It is one of the few ads that still exists, though its colonial origin has not been established. It is found in various places, including Vail's "Along the Hudson in Stage-Coach Days" (1905) and Earle's *Stage-Coach and Tavern Days* (1900).

Customers; and intends by unabated Diligence to merit a Continuance of their Favours. December 15, 1769."

Where Morse sourced this is unknown. Perhaps it came from local knowledge handed down, perhaps he had the (now long-lost) newspaper or perhaps it was indeed copied from this ad. For roughly a two-hundred-year period, from 1708 to 1908 when his book was published, there was nothing else preserved he could rely on to show there was a "Traphagen Tavern" or that the Traphagens were even innkeepers. Even after Morse's book, from 1908 to the present day, another one hundred or so years, nothing new has ever been uncovered. Some single reference should exist if there was any validity to the claim. Morse is also the sole source of there ever being a "Bogardus Tavern." (All Smith says on the topic is that "Bogardus was a merchant here and probably an innkeeper also.")

OTHER TALES

There are other tales of a few more legendary figures visiting or living at the BA. General Montgomery, who had a house in town, is said by Morse and Welles to have lived at the BA before his ill-fated campaign to Canada. President Martin Van Buren, from nearby Kinderhook, is said to have been a frequent visitor. There is little doubt some famous people stopped by the BA. Unfortunately, if not specifically written about in some newspaper, official record, BA register or some journal/diary, there is just no way to gauge the accuracy of such claims. Furthermore, while notable people stopping at the BA might be worth mentioning, it would be better to know if something significant occurred during their visit or even just which room they stayed in. The preserved record is virtually silent on these facts.

CHAPTER 8

The Early 1800s

Potter and Jacques

The relative peace and new sense of freedom that followed the Revolutionary War set in motion a period of optimism and exploration. People were on the move. The stagecoach and steamship businesses were gaining momentum. Trade, families, products, ideas and the unfortunate consequences of growth (a serious yellow fever epidemic occurred in New York in 1803) were spreading. James Monroe and Rhinebeck/Clermont's Robert R. Livingston negotiated the Louisiana Purchase in 1803. Lewis and Clark traveled across the continent from 1804 to 1806, and western expansion soon followed. The War of 1812 ran its course until 1815 (banded by two economic depressions, including the Panic of 1819, America's first financial crisis). John Adams, followed by Jefferson and then Madison, was elected to lead the young country. The Industrial Revolution from 1760 to roughly 1830 accelerated the production of goods and changed the world. In the arts, this was the age of Romanticism. Painting and literature were bursting with energy and meaning. On the Albany Post Road, coach and wagon traffic was noticeably increasing, and Rhinebeck's population had by now reached 3,662 souls, including 514 families and 421 slaves.[127] By 1834, the village was so well established that it formally incorporated.

As the country evolved and transitioned, so did the business at the corner. When Everardus passed away in 1799, his debt situation forced a public auction of his estate. His son Benjamin and wife, Maria, were living in Kingston by now, so it does not appear they intended to take control of the family business. Likely in a deal prearranged with the next owner, local innkeeper Asa Potter, Benjamin was able to win the auction and then immediately sell the property to Potter.[128] Potter was a highly respected young businessman in town. He came to Rhinebeck in 1787 from South Kingston, Rhode Island, and operated as early as 1788 as a merchant and trader, buying horses and exporting them to foreign markets.[129] By 1798, he appears to have owned his own tavern in town on Montgomery Street (across from Platt Avenue, the site of, or very near, Trimper's Tavern). It is possible he saw the larger Bogardus structure, situated at a better location, as a better business opportunity. Asa took control of the building and Bogardus's eighty-one acres on October 7, 1802. With the transition to Asa Potter, we also see for the very first time the labeling of the building as a business of any sort. The 1802 turnpike map has the label "Hotel" placed next to the BA.

Potter apparently made the first notable improvement: the north wing. Morse tells us: "The frame portion on the north end was erected by Asa Potter as a store." This may be true, as the 1810 Cox survey map shows the hotel with an extension. Halleck Welles also mentions that it was added around 1810 (both comments were possibly based on this map). This wing would eventually turn into the lobby/front desk for the hotel, a function it served until at least 1959. When used as a store, Smith mentions that "dry goods, groceries, and hardware [were sold] at different times."

Unfortunately, Potter passed away in October 1805 at the young age of thirty-nine. He left behind a wife and several children. The inn's ownership was transferred via a will ("to be held in trust for Asa's wife and children") to Asa's brother, Elisha R. Potter, from South Kingston, Rhode Island. Elisha held it for the next twenty-seven years, from November 25, 1807, until November 11, 1834.[130]

Elisha finally sold the BA in 1834 to New York City merchant Richard Schell, but Schell only held it until 1837, when he sold it to Jonathan Wilson. Wilson died soon after, and the property was probated and sold by court officer David Seymour back to Elisha's son, Elisha R. Potter Jr. This Elisha held it from September 7, 1839, until May 1, 1845 (another five and a half years). Through these roughly thirty-three years of Potter ownership and the five years in between, the hotel was leased out and managed by others. It is no surprise: both Elishas, father and son, were active attorneys, and each served for some time as Rhode Island's representatives to Congress.

Leasing in this era, and in this particular region, was likely viewed differently than we view leasing today. People were accustomed to this arrangement, given the complex and historical way land was held in the

The first dated sketch of the BA that is known to exist comes from this very rare masthead from an old December 25, 1849 *Rhinebeck Gazette*. *Author's collection.*

New York colony. The records show agreements that were "life leases plus one generation" and other long-term contract lengths. For the lessee, it was not quite ownership, but it was as close as it could be. In the early days, lease payments were a few schillings or simple commodities, such as bushels of "marketable wheat" or "one couple of fat hens" a year. Ownership arrangements did change slowly over time as a matter of practicality and changes-in-law. By the 1850s, the old system had almost completely shifted over to private land-ownership.[131]

THE JACQUES HOTEL

The most notable landlord family during the Potter ownership tenure went by the name of Jacques (or Jaques). This family took over management from 1805 until 1837, with the last two years run by the widow Jacques.[132] The Jacqueses brought the hotel its first real name and notability. By 1810, they seem to have turned the BA into a significant stagecoaching house. We will rely on Morse for most of this brief tale, as his version is the only one available. Morse was born in 1842, a little too late for the Jacques era, but still reasonably contemporary. He probably listened to stories from his parents' generation about the Jacqueses. Morse tells us:

In early life, Jacques had been captain of a river sloop. His boating experience proved a valuable asset. He was tall, broad, muscular and had a commanding presence. His force of character was great; his will power strong; his speech sharp and decisive; his manner genial; his action quick and positive. His physical powers were large; he could lift a heavy barrel of cider by the chimes and carry it into the cellar. He deserved and received respect from all. He admirably filled the very difficult position of tavernkeeper during stirring and trying times and until failing health forced him to retire. He was for more than a quarter of a century in the harness.

This, too, during an eventful period in the history of the State and nation. The second war with Great Britain was fought. Rhinebeck sons did their duty in this war. The Schells, De Lamaters, Platts, were then on the flatts. Martin Van Buren became the "Sage of Kinderhook," filled many State offices up to governor; then United States senator, minister, vice-president, and finally reached the goal, the presidency. He and his political friends were frequent guests of Jacques. The "old hotel" was a rendezvous for politicians. By the way of Rhinebeck, his trusted followers easily reached him.

Peter R. Livingston of "Grasmere" was also a leader of note. He had a national reputation. He was at the tavern almost daily. It was a headquarters for his friends. Gen. Armstrong lived there for a time. This period was the heyday of the road traveler, horseback rider, the stage coach and the post road. Rhinebeck village was a thriving and growing community. The tavern was a powerful magnet. The "White Corner" was built.

The frame annex to the hotel was rebuilt first for an enlarged store but soon afterwards, because of increasing business, it was used for hotel purposes. The "old hotel" kept pace with the times. "Aunt Polly" (Mrs. Jacques), assisted by her handsome daughters, was queen of the establishment; her son, Benjamin, was clerk; "Dinah" ruled the kitchen, and black Joe looked after the stables. The equipment was perfect in every detail. Rhinebeck, soon after the advent of the steamboat, became an important market town. Two barges made weekly trips to New York City. Market day drew crowds to the village; its trade drained the northern and eastern sections of the county. Jacques' tavern was the headquarters of drovers, traders, buyers and sellers for many years.

John L. Krimmel's circa 1820 *Barroom Dancing*, showing a scene that may have been similarly played out in the Jacques era of the "Old Hotel." *Library of Congress.*

Halleck Welles further describes William Jacques in his *Reminiscences of the Oldest Hotel in America 1700–1907*, writing, "He took the property over in 1805 and for 30 years was a noted figure in the community because of his rugged honesty, his great physical strength and sarcastic wit." Welles provides the anecdote: "The sign of the inn swung from poles at the south east corner. In 1812 a detachment of troops en route to invade Canada camped for the night in a grove of locusts close to the hotel, where the town hall now stands. Jacques offended the soldiers in some way, so during the night they cut down the sign. Next day he hung it high between two large locust trees in the grove and defied the whole army to cut it down. There it remained until his death, in 1835."

There is also an old story that on August 18, 1807, when the North River Steamboat (later referred to as the Clermont) finally passed Rhinebeck on its demonstration voyage from New York City to Albany, "one man, entering Jacques Tavern…took a stiff drink and claimed that he had just seen 'the devil going up the river on a sawmill.'"[133]

William Jacques passed away on October 29, 1835, at age sixty-seven.[134] Toward the end of the Jacques era, Elisha Potter decided to sell. This was when the hotel passed to a number of short-term owners before it came back to Elisha Jr. through the court system.

After the Jacques era came the brief tenure of Jacob Tremper as a leasing landlord. Continuing from Morse, "In 1837 Jacob H. Tremper became the landlord, with 'Wash' Nichols, clerk. Tremper became better known afterwards as 'Capt. Jake' of the Romer & Tremper Steamboat Company of Rondout. He was popular and successful in the 'old hotel,' but preferred steamboating." This Jacob Tremper was likely a descendant of the earlier Jacob Trimper/Tremper in town. Demonstrating his popularity, "Jacob H. Tremper" shows up as the name of a Central Hudson Line steamboat in 1918, so he did seem to find success on the river.[135] Morse continues:

> *In 1840 Tremper was succeeded by Robert T. Seymour, son-in-law of the well-remembered Capt. and Mrs. Jacques. A genial, popular, whole souled man, he knew how to run a hotel, and for fourteen years he did it. It was a jolly place during this period…A thriving village had come on the flatts. The Mexican war, the California gold fever, the hard-cider and Tippecanoe fight of 1840, the Clay-Polk battle in 1844, and the free-soil campaign of 1848 were exciting events, and the "old hotel" witnessed many notable gatherings of the clans…Gen. John A. Quitman, a Rhinebecker by birth, was a Mexican war hero, and the town furnished a dozen or more forty-niners. Seymour determined to "go west"; in 1853 the tavern had a new landlord, Oliver V. Doty, who remained for two years.*

This O.V. Doty is listed in a December 21, 1854 *Rhinebeck Gazette* ad as the proprietor of the Forbus House in Poughkeepsie (which became the Nelson House in 1876), so he may not have lasted the entire two years that Morse states. On May 1, 1845, in the middle of the Seymour lease era, Garret Van Keuren, William Platt and Henry Delamater bought the old hotel from Elisha Potter Jr. for $3,000. Van Keuren was the business manager and confidential agent of Morgan Lewis and the Livingstons (as well as heir to Springbrook, the estate that became the Dutchess County Fairgrounds).

A 1854 ad from the NYS Archives microfilm collection of the *Rhinebeck Gazette/American Mechanic.* The 1851 ad is from the July 19, 1851 *New York Daily Tribune,* Library of Congress Collection. Both are facsimiles of originals done for clarity.

FOR SALE.

THE **Hotel**, together with about **2** Acres of Land occupied by Robert T. Seymour in this village, is offered for sale. Application may be made to either

GARRET VAN KUREN,
WM. B. PLATT, or
H. DELAMATER.

Rhinebeck, July 27.

RHINEBECK HOTEL.

RHINEBECK N.Y.

The proprietor having thoroughly renovated and newly furnished this hotel is prepared to receive guests, and guarantees the comforts of home, with location and service unsurpassed. Carriages will be in readiness to convey guests to any desired place.

D. F. Sipperley, Proprietor.

June 22, 1854

RHINEBECK HOTEL. – The proprietor respectfully announces to his friends and the traveling community that he has thoroughly refitted his house, and that no pains will be spared to render its accommodations worthy its pleasant location and past reputation as one of the best Village Hotels in the State. His rooms are large, airy and comfortably furnished, and several families and single boarders may still be accommodated. Persons residing in cities and wishing to spend a portion of the Summer season in the country, will do well not to overlook Rhinebeck and its "rural attractions." His carriages are at all times in readiness to convey passengers to and from the boats (the River being two miles distant) or drive them into the country. The house is supplied with attentive servants, and the table with substantials and delicacies of the season, and every exertion made to render the visits of its guest pleasant.

EDWARD PULTZ

Rhinebeck, July 16, 1851

The Rhinebeck Hotel with patriotic bunting. Image is undated, but by now, the third floor has been added. Welles mentions an 1865 date for third-floor renovations. The motorcycle in the bottom left dates this photo to the early 1900s. *Courtesy of the MRH.*

The Rhinebeck Cornet Band in 1879. This picture hangs in the lobby of the BA with a list of its members. Rhinebeck was once the home of several seriously competitive bands and major music conventions were held in town (often getting front-page publicly in the *Rhinebeck Gazette*). *Courtesy of the Beekman Arms.*

William Platt and Henry Delamater were local White Corner merchants and future Bank of Rhinebeck presidents.

The trio appears to have tried to sell the BA right away, running ads in the *Rhinebeck Gazette* in 1846, but they were unsuccessful. They ended up holding it for eleven years, with Seymour as landlord and then Doty, who was then followed by David F. Sipperly.

Morse tells us that Sipperly was a brother-in-law of Martin L. Marquart, who was the next owner of the old hotel. Marquart purchased it from Van Keuren, Platt and Delamater on April 7, 1856, for $5,250. Edward Pultz followed Sipperly as landlord, and then Hunting Germond bought the hotel from Marquart on May 3, 1859, for $5,000 and succeeded Pultz. Each of these last four landlords (including Germond as owner) only ran the hotel for a year or two before they left. An official train stop at Rhinecliff came in 1854, but this was a difficult time in the country. The economy was overextended, leading to the Great Panic of 1857 (a major bank run). Abolition and secession were the talk of the day, as were other issues, such as the impact of the Irish potato famine (1845–52) and mass immigration. Everyone was worried about what was to come.

During this time, another world-changing event would occur. On August 28, 1859, George Bissell and Edwin L. Drake struck oil near Titusville, Pennsylvania. Oil was first used as an illumination fuel (distilled into kerosene). Manufactured coal gas had been employed sparingly by the 1820s (Rhinebeck had its own plant by at least 1879), but it was expensive, not universally available and was very dangerous.[136] There was still a strong demand for beeswax and tallow candles as well as for whale oil. (The whaling industry was at its peak level of activity in the 1850s, and it ran to the early 1900s. Quite remarkably, local whaling fleets sailed from Hudson's Claverack Landing, Poughkeepsie and Newburgh.) With a less expensive and more abundant fuel supply (refined oil), lights could be kept on longer. Extending the day increased productivity. People could do more, which fostered knowledge gathering and innovation. The world took a step forward. Soon, new ways to further refine the product would come, and new technologies would be developed to make use of this vast, storable, energy supply. Before all this happened, however, the country would go through a very turbulent period.

The Civil War descended on the nation in 1861. Before the 1863 draft was instituted, Rhinebeck raised regiments of the 20th Militia, 80th New York Infantry and 44th New York Infantry. After the draft, the town raised parts of at least three other companies—Company C of the 128th Regiment (in which author Howard Morse served as lieutenant) and Company F and Company K of the 150th Regiment. Nothing is noted about the BA's involvement as a recruiting post or rallying point, but it seems likely it played some role.

CHAPTER 9

The Mid- to Late 1800s

By the time of the Civil War, the long-haul stage operation from New York City had already become a romantic memory. The railroad was now dominating the north–south route and wartime spending was starting to stimulate the economy. With the train came a new generation of peddlers; this was the era of the traveling salesman. Though the trade started years earlier via horseback, it exploded as travel and resupply logistics became much more efficient. These "drummers" as they were called (their goal was to drum up business), found a home at the BA. You would have found a "drummer's table" in the dining room, where they would sit and share business leads and road experiences before the business of the day started. These salesmen would come to the BA, display their products and advertise their stay. Cigars, ladies' wear, musical instruments, brushes—almost anything and everything, both wholesale and retail, likely came by way of the old hotel.

At the BA, Hunting Germond, owner/landlord since 1859, apparently wanted out. In 1860, he gave the innkeeping duties to Burnett M. Conklin and Conklin's father-in-law, Lansing T. Mosher, a tavern keeper from Milan. Germond then sold the hotel on May 1, 1861, to James McElroy for $6,500, and McElroy took over as innkeeper. It seems to have changed to the "McElroy Hotel" with this transition. Morse provides a contemporary view of the era:

> *The Lincoln-Douglas canvas of that year stirred the old town as never before, and brought to the front two of the town's most prominent citizens:*

A typical announcement of traveling salesmen who would travel hotel-to-hotel selling goods to both wholesale merchants and retail buyers. *Rhinebeck Gazette*, March 23, 1863. Conklin ad in the January 28, 1862 *Rhinebeck Gazette* (it must have been running since September 1859). *Both found in the RHS collection, used with permission.*

Hon. William Kelly of Ellerslie, who became the Douglas candidate for governor, and Hon. Ambrose Wager, who was named on the same ticket for Congress. Worthy, deserving men, with hosts of supporters. Partizans joined the "Little Giants" or "Wide-A wakes," according to their political faith, and a battle royal was waged daily until election. The "old hotel" was, per force, neutral ground, and for weeks prior to election day was filled with visiting citizens from the north, south, east and west. Circumstances made it a storm centre. Excitement ran high in town, county, State and nation, and did not wane when the result was known, for then the dark cloud of Civil war commenced to spread, and as the "old hotel" completed a century of existence, the country was engulfed in bloody conflict, and Rhinebeck boys went forth to do battle for the integrity of the Union and the defense of the flag of our country.

After just three years of running the old hotel, McElroy sold his business to Griffin Hoffman on May 2, 1864, for $9,000.[137] Hoffman brought significant change to the BA. Morse tells us about Hoffman: "He had been a successful farmer, and was possessed of some means. He made extensive improvements; placed lawns, flower beds and walks in front; planted trees, using what had been the road in earlier times for the purpose, giving the entrance a yard appearance. He reconstructed the building, making sleeping rooms on the upper floor. He sold to the town the plot on the south where the town hall now stands." (Roughly sixty-five years later, it would be pulled down to make way for the new post office.) A bill of fare saved from the time that Hoffman operated the inn lists dinner for seventy-five cents, liquor for ten to twenty-five cents a drink and a room for the night for seventy-five cents.[138]

Six days after Hoffman purchased the BA, on May 8, 1864, the "Great Fire of Rhinebeck" tore through town, hitting the block across the Post Road (Mill Street) from the BA the hardest. Morse includes an etching in his book of the effort put in to suppress the fire. A bucket brigade starting from the town pump in front of the BA was organized to bring water to the flames. After the fire, a significant amount of rebuilding was required. The "rebirth" of the town may have been what inspired Hoffman to make the improvements to his hotel and the village corner.

A year later, on April 9, 1865, General Lee surrendered in Appomattox, and the Civil War was over. The April 11, 1865 *Rhinebeck Gazette* describes the day in Rhinebeck: "The news of Lee's defeat and the capture of Richmond was received in our village on Monday night of last week and made our whole population delirious with joy…The Rhinebeck band paraded our streets, the people kindled bonfires, rang bells, shouted, fired crackers, cannons and guns, and in many ways testified their joy at the good news."[139] One can just imagine this activity circling around the BA. Interestingly, Rhinebeck's 150th Regiment, battle-tested at Gettysburg, Chattanooga and in Sherman's assault on Georgia, was still in the middle of a battle in Goldsboro, North Carolina, when the town was celebrating. Its enemy did not capitulate until April 26.[140]

Hoffman stayed until 1873, and then he sold the property to the "Tremper Brothers." Smith wrote in his *History of Rhinebeck*: "It was rebuilt a few years since and greatly enlarged and is now kept by the Tremper Brothers, a first class hotel." (His history had skipped over everything since the Jacques, and this statement likely is referring to the Hoffman changes.) The Tremper brothers—actually George Clinton Tremper and his two nephews, brothers Harry and Alvin—did well at first, running a respectable business. George (born 1812) was a cousin of the Jacob who ran the old hotel briefly from 1837 to 1840 and was another seafaring Tremper. At one point in his life, George was captain of the horse-drawn ferry from Kingston to Rhinecliff.[141]

This was the gilded age after the Civil War, and the next generation of wealthy New Yorkers was creating their grand estates in Rhinebeck at the time.

Directly across from the BA and still in existence, this corner block was rebuilt at some point after the fire in 1864 and first served as the "Eagle Hotel." Below are the "Boots & Shoe Store" and at the corner, "Linden's Lager Beer & Billiard Hall." The town pump can be clearly seen. The hotel was here after 1867 but was gone by 1895. Another hotel, the "Union Hotel" shows up two lots south of the BA in 1858 then disappears. The 1900 and 1905 Sanborn maps show a "Keegan's Hotel" where the law offices are now located between Oak & Garden (site of the old dwelling). It later opened in 1907 as the Manhattan Restaurant.

In many cases, they were tearing down the old mansions of the Livingston era and rebuilding bigger ones. It was a strange time, as vast divides between rich and poor were opening up. The Great Panic of 1873 had just occurred, wiping out those who were not insulated. Yet another major financial crisis, the worst ever to date, began in 1893. For those who persevered and figured out how to profit and build wealth during this era, these were halcyon days in Rhinebeck.

Halleck Welles noted: "In the term of the Tremper Brothers occupancy the Rhinebeck Club was formed by the leading residents of the town including J.B. and Lewis Livingston, William Astor, Douglas Merritt, Wm. Bergh Kip, Robt. B. Huntington and a select few who loved the environments of the old hostelry and for five years used two of its large rooms as their club house."

Toward the end of their reign, the Trempers rang up too much debt operating the hotel, and they had their mortgage foreclosed on. Griffin Hoffman had to come back in and assume ownership again, now eleven years later. He ended up buying it back at a public auction on February 8, 1884, for $15,000. Hoffman hired the well-liked and experienced innkeeper Lorenzo Decker to run the hotel. Decker came from the Myers House (today's Stissing House) in Pine Plains. Harry Tremper shows up again in 1890 starting a company to explore for gold in the Rock City area of Rhinebeck. Alvin passed away in 1881 before the foreclosure.[142] Morse provides more contemporary comment on this era:

> *While he* [Decker] *was in charge, in 1888, the Harrison-Morton campaign gave Rhinebeck a boom. Levi. P. Morton, a resident, was the candidate for vice-president. He was then living at "Bois Dore," a few yards from the "old hotel." When notified of his nomination Gen. Harrison was with him, and the "old hotel" was filled as never before with representative men from all parts of the country. Harrison and Morton were elected, and for four years the second office, in rank, was ably filled by a Rhinebecker. In 1894 Mr. Morton, who then resided at Ellerslie, was nominated and elected governor of the State, and again "ye olde town" was crowded with statesmen of more or less prominence both before and after the election. Most of them were entertained at the "old hotel." Gov. Morton made an ideal executive, and was the choice of his State in 1896 for the presidency.*

This was also an interesting time in the history of Rhinebeck due to a new crop: violets. In 1886, the Saltford brothers launched Rhinebeck's violet industry in five greenhouses near the railroad. The Saltfords and other growers drove the town's violet production so high that the town proclaimed itself the "violet capital of the world." By 1900, 20 percent of Rhinebeck's 1,600 residents were employed in the violet industry, and it was rumored Rhinebeck had almost as many greenhouses as residential buildings. By World War I, tastes and priorities changed, and the industry declined. During its twenty-five- to thirty-year run, the economic impact on Rhinebeck was significant. Presumably, a fair amount of buyers, sellers, transporters and other suppliers passed through the old hotel during these years.

Opposite, top: New steamroller, May 1905, purchased to help bring paved roads to Rhinebeck in the budding automobile age. The photo appeared in the May 20, 1905 *Rhinebeck Gazette* with the names of those present. Vernon Lake, proprietor of the Rhinebeck Hotel (and Village Trustee), is third from the left. *Courtesy of the RHS.*

Opposite, bottom: "William M. Sayre Steamer Co." in front of the Rhinebeck Hotel in 1873, the year the company was organized. As late as 1896, there were four fire companies in town, each having roughly thirty to fifty members. There probably was not even a thought given to sweeping the street before this historic photo was taken. *Courtesy of the MRH.*

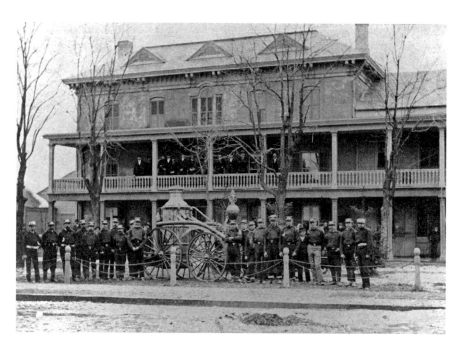

Another brief but notable event in its day occurred in August 1896. William Jennings Bryan, the three-time candidate for president and a leader in the Democratic Party came to visit Republican governor Morton at Ellerslie (Morton's home in Rhinecliff) on August 19. Bryan stopped at the BA for dinner and gave an impromptu speech. He was a popular figure in his day, and the event was picked up in newspapers all the way out to Denver. Bryan had an interesting platform, standing for women's suffrage, prohibition, trust-busting and anti-Darwinism (Bryan was the prosecutor in the famous 1925 Scopes trial).

When Hoffman passed away, his will executors sold the BA to Robert Hoffman, Nicholas Hoffman and Catherine Fulmer on May 1, 1889, for $10,000. Landlord Decker left in 1891 after seven years of running the hotel to open a competing inn in town. The owners then hired Edward Lasher to run the hotel from 1891 to 1893 and then E.M. Vanderburgh from 1893 to 1894.[143] Vernon Lake took charge in 1894, and Fulmer (alone) ended up selling Lake the hotel on February 1, 1904, for $12,000. The April 7, 1894 *Rhinebeck Gazette* mentions: "The Rhinebeck hotel has been renovated and put in first class condition by the new proprietor, Vernon D. Lake." Morse tells us, "Mr. Lake was a popular host. Under his supervision the 'old hotel' prospered. Modern improvements were introduced, and up-to-date methods employed in the management. Automobiles came in vogue. Parties adopting this mode of travel kept the 'old hotel' filled with lively and merry guests. Good beds, good meals, good service at Lake's assured a full house. Ill health forced Mr. Lake to retire."

On October 19, 1906, the Lakes sold the hotel to Halleck Welles for $21,000. Not much is known about Halleck, but during his brief tenure, he wrote a ten-page marketing booklet called *Reminiscences of the Oldest Hotel in America, 1700–1907*. It is historically inaccurate on most of the things he mentions, but it is one of the few older pieces of BA ephemera that still exists.[144] In the March 12, 1907 *Rhinebeck Gazette,* Welles announced that he converted the old sitting room (today's main lobby) into "an eighteenth century apartment." He also posted an ad in the August 17, 1907 *Rhinebeck Gazette* seeking old dishes, antiques and other decorations he could use at the Rhinebeck Hotel, so he seems to have been filled with the spirit of its history.

His brief one-year ownership is therefore surprising. When Halleck left, he moved back to Center Moriches, Long Island, got married and then "equipped" another hotel.[145] Perhaps he just found the hotel of his dreams. He visited Rhinebeck several times after leaving.

CHAPTER 10
The Turn of the Century

While the century opened somberly with President McKinley's assassination in 1901, sweeping innovation and change would soon come and define this era. Electricity reached Rhinebeck that same year. Marconi's first wireless transmission and the Wright brothers flight would become news. The Ford Motor company and several other auto manufacturers duly formed, and the "age of the automobile" had started. The country drive, promoted ever since the AAA formed in 1902, became a new leisure activity, and the BA proudly tacked above its front door a sign showing its AAA affiliation. The July 3, 1909 *Rhinebeck Gazette* noted, "More than 30 guests were registered at the Rhinebeck Hotel Wednesday night. The famous house is becoming a popular resort for automobile tourists."

After only a year of owning the BA, Halleck Welles decided to sell. Connecticut hotel manager Arthur Shuffle stepped in and bought it from Halleck on November 26, 1907, for $25,000. Shuffle ran it quietly, and barely a mention of him is made in the local papers. He ran ads in the *Brooklyn Daily Eagle* newspaper to try to get some of the New York City crowd to vacation in Rhinebeck. In the local August 3, 1912 *Rhinebeck Gazette*, he is cited for a number of fire violations he needed to fix, including putting in exit stairs and "remov[ing] the gasoline machine in his rear hall to the basement or outside of the building." In December 1912, a group of suffragist marchers made an address in front of the hotel and then had lunch inside. In February 1913, Shuffle advertised "a complete renovation and modernization" with the "installation of electricity and steam heating."

GRAND FAIR

OF THE

RHINEBECK FIFE, DRUM, AND BUGLE CORPS

TUESDAY TO SATURDAY

FEB. 17-18-19-20-21, '14

RHINEBECK TOWN HALL
BENEFIT CONVENTION FUND

Tuesday-Grand Opening Night
Wednesday-Drum Corps Night
Thursday-Firemen's Night
Friday-The Great Serpentine Dance
Saturday-Final Prize Contest

$2 Door Prize Each Night

Dancing

Music-von der Linden's Orchestra

Refreshments   Admission 15¢

RHINEBECK HOTEL

RHINEBECK, N.Y.

THE OLDEST HOTEL IN AMERICA

Thoroughly up-to-date
With Good Service.

Meals Served at All Hours

Open Night and Day.

Has Been Thoroughly Renovated
Local and Long Distance Telephone in Every Room.
PARTIES CATERED TO.

American and European Plan

Arthur Shuffle, Prop.

Shuffle advertisement in the February 14, 1914 *Rhinebeck Gazette. Found in the RHS collection, used with permission. A facsimile of the original ad used to provide clarity.*

In 1910, the Hub Garage, a stalwart Rhinebeck business that lasted until at least the mid-1960s, started behind the BA. Pete Snyder and Dick Turton were the owners, filling and servicing cars for both the passing public and for hotel guests. In these early days of the open automobile, they also offered the highly desired service of storing cars overnight.

Two years later, in April 1912, the sinking of the *Titanic* would shock Rhinebeck. On board was John Jacob Astor IV, a leading resident of Rhinebeck. Astor and 1,513 others perished in the disaster. The Astor influence in town, particularly in their real estate consolidation, would take a new course.

An article in a local paper during the Shuffle era describes the hotel's traditional annual opening:

Rhinebeck Hotel, from a card postmarked 1905. Note the pump, stage wagon near the north door and the relaxing gentlemen on the porch. *Author's collection.*

Possibly circa 1914 with the motorized coach now starting to appear. *Author's collection.*

A view of looking west down West Market Street, 1906. The Rhinebeck Hotel is to the left. *Author's collection.*

Postcard from the early 1900s looking south down Mill Street (the Albany Post Road). The BA is to the right. The sign above the street says 1700 STOP 1909, Arthur Shuffle, Prop, Oldest Hotel in America, Rhinebeck, NY. You can see the Hub Garage signs to the right (the garage was located just behind the BA). The women are standing in front of the pump. *Author's collection.*

Undated postcard, looking north. Shows signage for Hub Garage behind the BA, which opened in 1910. The town pump can just barely be seen at the corner. *Author's collection.*

Early 1900s, unidentified car (possibly a Hudson based on the hubcaps' emblems) in front of the old Rhinebeck Hotel. Looks like they have the heat turned on (blankets & gloves). *Courtesy of the RHS.*

Harlem Valley Times, Amenia, N.Y. May 24, 1913
FAMOUS OLD DUTCHESS COUNTY HOTEL OPENS
Two Hundred and Thirteenth Season Opens with Dinner at Rhinebeck

With music and decoration and one of the most elaborate dinners ever served in Rhinebeck, the famous old Rhinebeck Hotel (the oldest point of service in America) opened its 213th summer season on Wednesday says the Rhinebeck Gazette. Landlord Arthur Shuffle has issued invitations to the porch dinner and guests to the number of nearly fifty enjoyed his hospitality. Vonder Linden's orchestra furnished the music for the occasion and began playing at 7:30 o'clock. The music continued while the guests assembled throughout the evening.

During the past few months many improvements have been made at the hotel and the upper porch had been lighted by electricity. The tables

Early 1900s chain-driven "horseless stage." The Fraleigh Brothers (F.J. and John) stagecoach line was the last to exist in Rhinebeck, having taken over Matthias Wortz's stage and stable in December 1899. Their business was on West Market Street, just outside of the north door of the BA. *Courtesy of the RHS.*

were placed on the porch. They were decorated with tulips and were most attractively spread.

The "213th" claim takes you back to 1700, which of course was simply marketing spin, though by this point the old hotel was likely showing its age. Renovations were made in 1865, 1872, 1894, 1904 and 1913, but the "modern age" was upon Rhinebeck, and others had visions for a different, grander approach.

The Shuffles sold in 1914, and soon after, the BA was forever changed. Mr. Shuffle passed away at age fifty-three, in 1915. Mrs. (Annie) Shuffle surfaced as the owner of the Rhinecliff Hotel, also in 1915. (Mr. and Mrs. Shuffle purchased it on December 14, 1911, and had been running both hotels at the same time.) An August, 4, 1915 *Rhinebeck Gazette* article notes Mrs. Shuffle was involved in a hard-fought lawsuit against the town and

Business meeting in the new south wing of the BA in 1919. Old newspapers are filled with notices of meetings and activities held at the BA, from political rallies, to fire company dances, to public auctions of real estate. Today, this room hosts many of the activities during the winter Sinterklaas Festival. This room was completely renovated in 2012. *Courtesy of the RHS.*

New York Central Railroad. Apparently the railroad, with the town's approval, blocked the properties' entrance to the river, so she sued for substantial damages and won. Town taxpayers were not particularly happy with the outcome.

CHAPTER 11

The Foster and Dows Renovations

O n November 16, 1914, Wallace "Wally" Foster of Kingston bought the Rhinebeck Hotel from Arthur Shuffle. Foster, former manager of the popular Eagle Hotel in Kingston, had big dreams for Rhinebeck. He immediately announced his plans to renovate the old hotel. The *Rhinebeck Gazette* declared on November 7, 1914: "The Rhinebeck Hotel will become the property of Wallace Foster of Kingston on Monday, Nov. 16. The new landlord will make several improvements to the building and expects to give the village a modern and attractive hotel."

Foster's early ownership coincided with the start of World War I (1914–18). Around the country, the wealth of the nation was slowly changing, as efficient manufacturing and a sustainable labor model both came into place. Prohibition would start in January 1919, along with the second year of a worldwide influenza epidemic. A postwar recession stalled the economy briefly, but President Harding's 1921–22 reforms, including the roll back of income taxes (which started in 1913), helped turn the country around. Soon, the "roaring '20s," a period of sustained economic and cultural growth, would start. Art Deco, flappers and jazz were in, and there was a new feeling that modern innovation could solve any problem. Improved automobiles, airline service, radio, motion pictures and penicillin (discovered in 1928) were among many things that would make life better for all.

During the war, Mr. Foster decided to expand. The formal announcement came in January 1917, likely when he finally found financing:

RHINEBECK HOTEL IS BEING ENLARGED
Rhinebeck Gazette, *January 13, 1917*
Work Began Monday—A Large Addition—Plans Drawn by H.T. Lindeberg—Landlord Foster Will Have Modern Hostelry

That "The Oldest Hotel in America" now has the prospect of being also one of the most inviting, hospitable, and comfortable hotels in the country is due to Mr. Wallace W. Foster's ambition and farsighted vision. The entire hotel is to be remodeled. Harry T. Lindeberg, the architect who designed the building of Holiday Farm, has completed his plans and it is hoped that work will finish by June first.

The design is a typical Colonial house, the front portico extending up two stories, a block tile terrace in front of the building extending the entire length, with a retaining wall; on the north side, a portecochere extending over the sidewalk, developing a north entrance on West Market Street. The old part of the house will be restored and kept old. A large wing will be built on the south, making a dining room with a seating capacity of one hundred people; and on the second floor six rooms. There will be a new enlarged kitchen, steam heat from a huge heating plant, rooms with connecting baths, and hot and cold water in all sleeping rooms.

For the present, the Luff building will be used as a modern and commodious laundry for the hotel. The new "Oldest Hotel in America" will be the culmination of Mr. Foster's career as a hotel manager, and proprietor. Mr. Foster has been in the hotel business since he was fifteen years old, and in that time has been associated with only two proprietors. When he bought the hotel here he saw the possibilities for it, and amid discouraging conditions of house and the servant problem, has nevertheless managed to conduct a good business and make the hotel attractive. His ambition for the new hotel—for it will be practically a new hotel, so great and so many are the changes—is to have an excellent cuisine, inviting dining room, luxurious bedrooms and baths, and all the comforts for which the traveling public longs, and is willing to pay.

Rhinebeck is fortunate that Mr. Foster chose this hotel in which to work for the realization of his ambition and dream. The entire village sympathizes with his effort, and will be proud of the new hotel which will soon rise on the old site.

Elise Lathrop, writing in her 1926 *Early American Inns and Taverns*, provides some commentary on what the BA was like before Foster purchased it: "It was then in a deplorable state, having been used as a common saloon, but he has restored and added to it so as to preserve the old style, replacing the ugly double piazzas with a pillared portico across the front…This inn, operated for six months of the year, is Rhinebeck's only ancient hostelry still in business."[146]

Foster also republished Halleck Welles's *Reminiscences of the Oldest Hotel in America* and tacked this to the end:

> *The present proprietor of the Inn, Mr. Foster, purchased the property in 1914, and has been constantly developing it along the best lines believing that there is a demand for the highest class accommodation and food from the large number of automobilists using the great tourist routes, the Inn being located at the intersection of the two greatest Hudson Valley routes as will be seen from the diagram on the back cover. The oldest hotel in America has been completely remodeled from plans of Harrie T. Lindeberg, the New York architect, and retains the charms of age and historic association with the added attraction of an up-to-date heating plant, many bathrooms and modern plumbing throughout the building.*

Near the time, or possibly even before, he acquired the hotel, Foster was acquainted with Tracy Dows, a wealthy New York City banker.[147] Dows became a Rhinebeck resident in 1903, having married the socialite Alice Olin, heir of Glenburn (a river estate in Rhinebeck). By 1910, Dows had finished the main part of his new estate, Fox Hollow, just south of town. Now that he had time, he may have been looking to do public good or make a business investment in the community. Dows and his friend, the renowned architect Harrie T. Lindeberg, certainly traveled through town to get a "feel for the place," and surely they had been reading *Gazette* articles keeping tabs with the local comings and goings (Jacob Strong, publisher of the *Gazette*, was also a friend of Dows). It is not clear how they were introduced, but at some point, Foster and Dows struck up a friendship. Soon after, visions were shared and agreements made. Through Dows, Foster connected with the City Real Estate Company on April 23, 1917, to obtain a $20,000 mortgage. This was roughly the market value of the property. Foster himself only paid Shuffle "$100 & other good & valuable consideration," possibly because the hotel was in need of serious work, but the specifics are not disclosed. (It must not have been that bad, as Shuffle advertised renovations and his own daughter got married there.) Photos in the Dows Collection show the old hotel starting to get pulled apart in April 1917. Construction must have been on an accelerated schedule, as the BA reopened on September 15, 1917. During the construction, workmen found an old army jacket in the walls that they believed was from the Revolutionary War.[148]

Like everything Tracy Dows was involved in, his influence extended to more than just financing.[149] He had an office in the second-floor north corner room of the BA. It moved across the street after the reconstruction, likely so he could have a view of his new grand enterprise. Interestingly, when the renovations were complete, Foster still called himself "proprietor," which connotes ownership, so control does not appear to have transferred completely.

Dows's daughter Deborah, in her recorded reminiscences, remembers "Wally" as "the first manager."[150] She also mentions that Wally used the barn and had two horses (she had one there as well). The pasture was right next to it to the south. Foster advertised in a November 27, 1915 *Rhinebeck Gazette* article that he had "several well trained saddle horses for hire and instruction would be given. W.W. Foster, Rhinebeck Hotel." (According to his obituary, Foster was an accomplished horseman, known throughout the Hudson Valley as a judge at shows and at harness races and county fairs in the state.) The barn we see now (which has been serving as an antique store since the LaForge days) was built just before Foster came into ownership. A November 12, 1902 *Rhinebeck Gazette* article mentions that the old barn "of Lake's Rhinebeck Hotel" caught on fire and burned to the ground at a loss of $4,000–$5,000.[151] Foster was not stuck in the age of horses, however. A September 8, 1916 *Rhinebeck Gazette* article announced, "W.W. Foster, the popular landlord of the Rhinebeck Hotel is driving a new Oldsmobile and Miss Anna Mitchell is the owner of a new 'Grant 6' runabout. Rhinebeck's auto population is continually increasing."

THE CREATION OF AN ICON

Many people have lamented the disappearance of the balconies on the front of the BA. Old recorded stories of dinner parties there describe meals being served on the balconies with flowers on the table and electric illumination above. Postcards of the day show visitors relaxing on the porches watching the world go by. A May 30, 1914 *Rhinebeck Gazette* article mentions, "The Rhinebeck Fife, Drum and Bugle Corps serenaded Mr. and Mrs. Gordon A. Holmes at the Rhinebeck Hotel on their return from their wedding trip Wednesday evening." One can just imagine them looking down from above on this interesting mix of music.

The dramatic renovations that took place would likely never be allowed in this day and age, but Foster and Dows pulled it off and changed the center of Rhinebeck forever. It is all we know. Fortunately, Harrie Lindeberg was probably the finest architect in the world at that time, and his design choices seem like they will pass the test of time (and, arguably, altering the BA was not as bad as pulling down the historic White Corner building across the street and turning that into a gas station in the 1940s). Lindeberg also designed the Astor Home for Children (formerly known

The recently completed and rechristened Beekman Arms, circa 1918, trying to get the grass to start growing. Old Glory hangs proudly above the new portico. The beautiful elms in front eventually succumbed to Dutch elm disease, which had reached Rhinebeck by 1959. They were taken down circa 1975. *Courtesy of Charles LaForge.*

Tracy Dows's Fox Hollow mansion, just south of the village, 1911, a year after it was finished (it exists today as a drug and alcohol treatment center). Bottom photo is the strikingly similar Beekman Arms from the 1940s. Architect Harrie T. Lindeberg favored the same "gentleman farmer" manor house/Colonial Revival style he used on Fox Hollow. *Photo above from the Dows Collection, courtesy of Hudson River Heritage; photo below courtesy of the MRH.*

as Holiday Farms), a few doors down the road and the Astor dairy barns. Of the BA, it is said architecture is a mirror that reflects the character of a people, so this restoration is very telling of what the owners and perhaps townspeople felt. A reverence for the past—and possibly a bit of blue-blooded pride—seems to show through.

The Liberty Ball being rolled down West Market Street by Scout troops. Image is undated, but an April 27, 1918 *Rhinebeck Gazette* article mentions the ball: "The Liberty Ball is a giant red, white and blue sphere, seven feet in diameter. The phrase 'keep the ball rolling' suggested it as a symbol of the Liberty Loan. Every subscriber to the third loan is privileged to help roll it onward. Everywhere it goes it is greeted with cheers and is pushed onto New York." *Courtesy of the MRH.*

Dows's Fox Hollow mansion itself was built in its own unique Colonial Revival style of architecture following the lines of Washington's Mount Vernon. Dows's direction to Lindeberg on Fox Hollow was that it should take on the look of a gentlemen's farm.[152] This country manor architectural style resonated with Dows, Lindeberg and Foster, so it is no surprise the Beekman Arms took on a very similar appearance.

A DIFFICULT TIME FOR THE HOTEL BUSINESS

The early part of the 1900s was an exciting but often difficult period in the United States. The unfolding of the Great War caused plenty of distractions detrimental to the hospitality business. Prohibition and the faltering postwar economy made things worse (the BA, bowing to pressure, went dry a year earlier in 1918). Even though the Roaring '20s were starting to steam through the metropolitan areas, the countryside was far less impacted by the hubris. Early postcards of the BA advertised that it was "open all year," but by 1919, we see that changed to "open May through November." Going "off-season" is how former landlords appeared to traditionally run the hotel. Foster seemed to try to keep it open all year, which just did not work out. Townspeople hated to see it close; it made Rhinebeck feel isolated. A November 13, 1920 *Rhinebeck Gazette* article states: "Beekman Square presents a desolate aspect with the oldest hotel in America closed and its blinds drawn. The hotel annex on West Market Street is now open for business." (Apparently, for a short time there was an annex used for any off-season lodging. The "Beekman Arms Annex" shows up on the 1923 Sanborn map on the east corner of Garden Street and West Market Street.)

Financial troubles would come for Foster. By 1925, he was ousted from the hotel, and foreclosure proceedings were started against him.[153] How, and under whom, the BA operated the next year in 1926 is not clear. It did close in October for the winter.

On April 27, 1927, the lender finally made it through the courts and foreclosed on Foster's 1917 mortgage because it had not been paid. At the forced sale, Dows's Foxhollow Development Corp. stepped in and paid $20,000 for the hotel property and the adjoining lots the Fosters owned. While Tracy Dows was the principal owner, this ownership group/corporate board also included F.C. Townsend, head of a CPA firm in New York City; Jacob Strong, editor of the *Gazette*; Peter Troy, a Poughkeepsie stockbroker; and Paul Gravenhorst, a prominent New York attorney. The ownership group (with members replaced over time) owned the BA for roughly another ten years before Dows's untimely death prompted changes.

Opposite, top: Tracy Dows, likely circa 1918. Tracy was instrumental in the complete renovation of the BA in 1917. He owned it from 1927 to 1937. Any partial ownership before this period is not documented. There likely was some quid pro quo arrangement between Dows (banker) and Wallace Foster (proprietor) from the start. By 1917, Dows had an office in the second-floor north corner room of the BA. His office moved across the street (Mill Street) in 1918, possibly so he could look out and view "his" grand newly renovated building. *The Dows Collection.*

Opposite, bottom: The old main lobby (in the north wing). This 1918 photo was taken from Tracy Dows's scrapbook. Note the tin walls and ceiling and the cigars being sold. Hunt club drawings seem to be the décor. *The Dows Collection.*

These were clearly difficult times at the BA. With a lack of business, there was no justification for keeping the building open. The BA closed again in the winter of 1927, but Dows did take the opportunity to do a "complete alteration" that year, "modernizing and redecorating" the building. Private telephones, running water and "in most cases a bath" were added to each room. In addition to the updating done, the owners also contracted with a group called Hotel Campbell Management to run the business. This group was led by George Campbell, a successful businessman and the ex-mayor of Poughkeepsie. Dows logically turned to associates he could trust to help turn the place around. Their first resident manager was Frank Lord, an experienced hotel man from New York City.

This arrangement did not last long. The BA closed again in the winter of 1929. By 1930, the Campbell Management Group was out, and the board of the Beekman Arms, Inc. had changed. The idea now was to keep management local. The following article ran in the April 19, 1930 *Gazette*:

LOCAL GROUP TO OPERATE HOTEL
BEEKMAN ARMS CORPORATION PLACES RHINEBECK MEN ON BOARD AT MEETING TUESDAY—TO OPEN MAY FIRST FOR "ALL THE YEAR"

Beekman Arms is now a corporation run by Rhinebeck men, for Rhinebeck's good and with a manager who is well known locally. Beekman Arms opens this year on May 1st as an All-Year-'Round Hotel with many new furnishings, and with a change of policy both as to restaurant and rates. These, in brief, are the announcements made, following the quarterly meeting of the corporation which was held Tuesday morning at Rhinebeck. Members of the board present included the President, Tracy Dows; Treasurer, Jacob H. Strong; F.C. Townsend and Paul G. Gravenhorst of New York City. After the transaction of routine business, the resignations of Messrs. Peter H. Troy, F.C. Townsend and Mr. Gravenhorst were presented, after the acceptance of which, a new trio of directors was named to complete the board.

To take the place of Mr. Townsend as Vice-President, Nelson Coon was named, while the places of the other two directors will be filled by Henry B. Cornelius and DeWitt Schermerhorn. Mr. Coon has, since the meeting, consented to act as Executive Vice President to handle the details of the Beekman Arms Corporation. This change in the membership of the board means that henceforth Rhinebeck's historic old hostelry will truly be the Rhinebeck Hotel. For many years past men who have been comparative strangers have conducted the affairs at the old Inn and for some

A 1917 renovation photo taken by Tracy Dows shows demolition in progress. The existing barn can be seen to the left, top photo. Below, in front is the temporary Hub Garage, placed there until new quarters could be secured across the street. *From the Dows Collection.*

time It has been thought to make such a change and with the termination of the agreements with the Campbell management, this plan was made a possibility. As announced previously in the Gazette, *the corporation has secured as managers of the Beekman Arms for the season about to open, two people who are well known to many folks here—Mr. and Mrs. Frank D. Cole—who have already taken up their abode at the hotel where they are superintending the annual housecleaning and a number of minor changes and improvements that will provide added comfort for the guests. One of the principal changes that will make the hotel of added value to the community at large is the decision to keep Beekman Arms open the year 'round. This will enable the spacious dining hall to be used as a gathering place for organizations, for dinner parties and dances during the winter months, the lack of which has been very keenly felt. No stone will be left unturned to make the Beekman Arms a truly local institution and plans are already being formulated to make the hotel a focal point of social activity. Special inducements will doubtless be made to various organizations to use the hotel more freely and during the summer months it is hoped that arrangements can be made to promote the use of the beautiful garden for afternoon fetes and already Director Schermerhorn is planning to serve his iced drinks on the spacious shaded terrace of the hotel. In spite of many of the improvements and changes that are being made, the price scale of both the rooms and meals will receive some downward revision with special attention being paid to the weekly and monthly rates for those desiring to spend the summer or live permanently In this delightful central spot. The opening day, as noted previously, will be Wednesday, May 1ˢᵗ, and the* Gazette *hopes to present next week more complete details of the improvements made and changes contemplated. Mr. and Mrs. Cole will be on hand to welcome their fellow citizens and a special menu will be provided for the day.*

After the Coles' brief summer tenure, Lewis Winne was hired in late 1930, and he seemed to start turning the business around.

THE LEWIS WINNE TENURE AT THE BEEKMAN ARMS

Winne came from Cheery Valley, New York, to run the hotel in the fall of 1930. This was in the midst of the Great Depression, a difficult time, but Winne took it on as a personal challenge to succeed. "I do

The old Hub Garage (left), icehouse (which stored ice from Crystal Lake down the street) and new bricks for the south wing piled high. The wing was designed to be wood, but insurance issues prompted a change. *From the Dows Collection.*

not believe in slumps," he proclaimed, saying they were "just the letting down of individual effort." He was a true salesmen and a very successful hotel manager, recognizing early what was important to drive business (he was the son and grandson of hotel managers). He began a three-prong approach to changing the culture and business prospects of the hotel. His first undertaking was to "sell himself to the people of the community, to the guests, to the employees, and to everyone concerned." He felt to be successful at his job, he needed people to see him as being confident. The second step he took was the implementation of a new aggressive marketing plan. "I determined I would cash in on the fact that the Beekman Arms was the oldest hotel in America," he said, and from here, he began weekly newspaper ads which spoke directly to readers. He also tied up deals with clubs, businesses and other organizations requiring space (even searching out future celebrations and writing letters to possible organizers). Another part of the marketing was to keep the hotel open and accessible, making local residents feel the hotel was a "community interest" and, consequently, they were all partners in its

The lobby (here called the sitting room) just after the Foster/Dows renovations, 1918. At this time, the working hotel lobby was in the north wing, where it had historically been, and would remain, until the early 1960s. The brand new BA sign is waiting to be hung outside. *The Dows Collection.*

Though one thinks of the Old Rhinebeck Aerodrome when looking at this picture, it is actually a 1931 picture promoting the "Air Meet Circus" at Cozine Field in town (now Knollwood Road near the elementary school). The plane is actually described as "modern" in a July 1, 1931 *Poughkeepsie Eagles-News* article. *Courtesy of the MRH.*

success. His third step was to figure out what the hotel did best and sell that the most (which was principally certain foods). He determined to have the best product on the market at the best price, and he wanted to make sure his customers felt like they were getting a good deal. Winne was so good at running the business, he claims to have increased sales 75 percent in the first month alone. A November 21, 1931 *Rhinebeck Gazette* article mentions the BA had already sold "7,000 more dinners than the previous year." He knew he had to keep it up to maintain his success, saying that "it was absolutely necessary to wage a vigorous sales campaign at all times," which he seems to have done (his scrapbooks are filled with his ads). His longevity is a testament of his success. Winne later became part-owner and he operated the hotel all through World War II.[154]

THE END OF THE DOWS ERA

Somewhat like Henry Ford with the Wayside Inn and John Rockefeller with Colonial Williamsburg, Tracy Dows had the financial clout and sensibilities to recharge the facility and keep it "cared for" properly when it needed it most. It is not right to say he saved the BA, as the attractive location probably would have brought someone else (and Foster had a say in it). Dows did leave his mark, and he will forever remain an important part of the BA's story. His influence in a way changed the soul of the Beekman Arms. From an old stage stop and simple functional hotel, it had been transformed into a prestigious grand landmark.

In addition to his work at the BA, Dows was also involved in local civic affairs. He helped move the Dutchess County Fair from Washington Hollow to Rhinebeck (said to be in 1919). He was on several town committees and was a director with the Rhinebeck Cemetery Association. He hired a photographer to record the historic structures in town (now part of the DAR collection, held by the RHS). He was also an active member of the Dutchess County Historical Society. As time went on, his family grew, found other interests and seemed to separate. In 1937, Tracy Dows, at sixty-five, decided to move to London. In July of that year, he unexpectedly passed away.

CHAPTER 12

Beekman Arms Inc. after Dows

Deborah Dows tells us in her recorded memoir that when Tracy died in July 1937, he left the "BA," as they called it, to his wife, and "Lewis Winne was running it then, so we just kept it going." Deb mentions that she thought about taking on the business but realized it was not for her. Neither her sister Margaret (married to a Swedish diplomat and living abroad) nor her brother Olin wanted it. Another major recession hit the country in 1937–38 (bringing 19 percent unemployment), probably changing their priorities. They eventually decided to sell in 1939. A group of eight local businessmen banded together to buy out the Dows and keep the old landmark in operation under their control (for $35,000 on November 14, 1939).[155] This group included Lewis F. Winne (serving as the first president), Pierre E. Cookingham (owner of the local hardware store, a lot south of the post office), Dr. Howard S. Bulkeley (beloved local doctor for whom the middle school was later named), local attorney Benson R. Frost, S. Richard Lloyd (owner of local Chrysler dealership), Dr. Kenneth Chase (a local dentist whose office was opposite the BA), A. Chester Haen (a local jeweler/clocksmith) and Olin Dows (Tracy's son).[156] Tracy Dows's Beekman Arms Inc. was dissolved, and a new Beekman Arms Inc. was reincorporated on December 19, 1939.

The early era of this management group was an important time in the life of the Beekman Arms. World War II was coming, and President Roosevelt, a Dutchess County native, was in office. FDR returned to the area as often as practical to visit his home in Hyde Park. While in the area, he also visited the surrounding local towns, including Rhinebeck. Not surprisingly, he

Ford's 28,000,000[th] Model A (a 1940 Ford Sedan) toured North America and stopped by the BA. To the far left is Lewis Winne. The gentleman with his foot on the bumper appears to be the Ford representative. He's seen in other photos of this car around the country. The two gentlemen to the right are identified by the RHS as the local Ford dealers. *Courtesy of the MRH.*

had several connections to town. The Delano families in Rhinebeck were relatives. Margaret (Daisy) Suckley, his confidante, lived here at Wilderstein, and his chauffeur, Monte Snyder, hailed from Rhinebeck. The August 31, 1934 *Rhinebeck Gazette* points out that he made annual visits to the Dutchess County Fair. Articles in the *New York Times* dated November 8, 1932, and November 2, 1936, describe his end-of-campaign visits to Rhinebeck (and in 1932, specifically to the Beekman Arms). A November 5, 1940 *Poughkeepsie Eagle-News* article mentions his seemingly standard pre-election day trip around the Dutchess County region. After speeches at the Nelson House in Poughkeepsie, FDR went down to Wappinger Falls, then to Beacon, across to Newburgh, up to Kingston and then back over to Rhinebeck, by which time he was utterly exhausted ("and so I am stopping here for a minute to say good evening…"). It seems he barely spent any time in Rhinebeck before going home to Hyde Park. It was very good that he came, but the BA, contrary to legend, was not FDR's special destination for political celebrations (though being the great politician that he was, he probably did make people feel that way). He did love Rhinebeck and the Beekman Arms. It was the BA that helped bring a notable federal works project to town.

FDR AND THE RHINEBECK POST OFFICE

After finishing the Poughkeepsie post office project, President Roosevelt turned to Rhinebeck. Rhinebeck was another early Dutchess County town with colonial roots and stone buildings, both strong motivating factors to him. (Other towns FDR later selected were Wappinger Falls, Ellenville and Hyde Park.)

Six Rhinebeck locations were considered. Benson Frost, a widely known Rhinebeck attorney, and Colonel Jacob Strong, publisher of the *Rhinebeck Gazette*, took the president on an inspection tour in 1937. By this time, the Kip-Beekman-Heermance house had already been destroyed by fire (1910), so Jacob Strong thought to bring the president by it to inspect the stone. FDR was familiar with this house and took a particular interest in it given his Beekman connection. After seeing it again in old photos, he wanted the new post office designed in its shape, using its stone.

The Beekman Arms factored into the final location decision. The *Poughkeepsie Star Enterprise* reported on November 3, 1937: "It has been reported that President Roosevelt in his tour of sites last Saturday expressed particular satisfaction with the building [the old town hall], being of the opinion, it was said, that the Beekman Arms would provide an attractive setting for the federal structure...The reports said that the site might also incorporate the building housing the Cookingham hardware store located south of the town hall." FDR's project manager then negotiated the purchase and use of the stone from the house with the Suckleys (owners of the ruined Beekman house property). There was not enough stone for the entire building, but they used what they could and procured other local stone to finish it (a quarry was on the eastern side of the property, and a number of outcroppings of similar stone in the area were identified). FDR stated in his dedication speech, "We have been able to incorporate much of the stone in the original Beekman house in the front walls of this Post Office." Part of the agreement was to leave the small circa 1708 eastern portion of the ruins standing, though from the full description, more was anticipated to stay than what still stands today. Just before construction, it seems at Daisy's urging, FDR had an idea to actually reproduce the entire larger original structure identically, including turning it

President Roosevelt and Crown Prince Frederik of Denmark and Iceland leaving the post office dedication on May 1, 1939. *Courtesy of the Franklin D. Roosevelt Presidential Library and Museum, Hyde Park, New York.*

ninety degrees. His architect talked him out of it at the end.[157] The post office was dedicated on May 1, 1939. To FDR's delight, Daisy donated the stone lintel from the original house with the 1700 date and Hendrick Kip's initials on it, as well as a sash and piece of glass with the etched signatures of two of the Livingston girls, "Katy Livingston jun" and "Margaret Livingston." Both are on display in the post office, along with other artifacts.

In FDR's dedication speech, he spoke directly to the people of Rhinebeck on his vision for the town center:

> *May I make a suggestion to you, my neighbors of Rhinebeck? At this very historic crossroads of the village we now have the new Post Office, the nation-wide famous Beekman Arms Inn, and just beyond it on the northwest corner that fine old stone building, so substantially built that it will last for all time to come* [White Corner, torn down the next year for a gas station]. *As time goes on, some of the other buildings on the other side of the street and on this side may have to be*

replaced by new buildings. Now, these buildings are substantial enough but they are set rather close to the street and represent a style of architecture that is not being copied much today, a style that was followed by architects for years but one which we now rather smile at as we label it Victorian.

And so, when replacements are made, I hope that the new buildings may be set back by—what shall we say?—not by law but by community opinion, set back so that you in Rhinebeck will have what, in effect, will be a large open square, admired for its beauty by the many thousands who pass this way.[158]

THE UNCERTAIN 1950S

The inn continued under the leadership group for roughly twenty-nine years, from 1940 to 1969. After Lewis Winne's tenure (late 1930–48) problems started again. The country had not quite fully adjusted back to a post–World War II peacetime economy before the Korean War and more uncertainty came along. The Cold War and nuclear threat, as well as the developing anti-segregation movement, were changing the country. Business was off, so winter hotel closings became common again. The January 19, 1950 *Rhinebeck Gazette* read, "For the first time in nearly twenty years, the Beekman Arms, oldest hotel in America, is closed temporarily to reopen when Winter is past." The BA went on to shut down in winters every year from at least 1950 to 1954, with an attempt to keep it open in 1952.

The group desired to lease out the BA long-term to someone who could turn it around, but it just could not find the right person. Winne was ill in 1949, so Harry Williams ran it that year. Ken Arnold became manager in 1950 (he had just come up from operating a hotel in the Bahamas and hoped to bring the BA international recognition). Howard Hohl tried leasing it in 1952, and Walter Harter, a very capable hotel man who was running another hotel up in Schoharie, New York, stepped in and leased it in 1954. Nothing was running smoothly. The April 29, 1954 *Rhinebeck Gazette* mentions: "The local owners of the Beekman Arms have been involved with management in civil suits and counter suits" (quite possibly due to the poor business climate and financial issues). The hotel kept closing in the winter. Townspeople were genuinely worried about the hotel's future. The *Rhinebeck Gazette* had to run a brief article on March 25, 1954, dismissing the rumor that the BA was to be torn down. Fortunately, by 1958, the BA would find direction.

CHAPTER 13

The Charles LaForge Era

"The Beek"

In 1957, a Cornell University School of Hotel Management student by the name of Don Blackburn heard about the Beekman Arms and came to the management group with a proposal to operate the hotel under a long-term lease. The businessmen carefully considered the proposal but, in the end, determined Blackburn was a bit too young and inexperienced. Roughly a year later, in July 1958, the ownership group contacted Blackburn and asked if he was still interested in running the hotel. Blackburn by now had acquired the Blacksmith Shop, a restaurant in Millbrook, New York, so he put the owners in touch with his best friend and Cornell classmate, Charles "Chuck" LaForge Jr. and their mutual friend James "Jim" Fahey. LaForge and Fahey had graduated from Cornell and at the time were leasing and operating the Skyline Inn in Manchester, Vermont. (Another Cornell graduate and classmate, George Banta, will figure prominently in the next chapter.)

Although he grew up in Monroe, New York, LaForge had never heard of the Beekman Arms. When he walked up to see it for the first time, he immediately knew it was for him. It needed some work, as it was "ramshackled, poorly managed, and not [a] very popular inn. The dining room contained pink plastic chairs and birds. Some birds were plastic, and some were live!"[159] The building was open and being used, but a full updating was required. When they agreed to take over as operators of the BA, LaForge and Fahey signed a ten-year lease with an option to buy. LaForge stated this is the best contract he ever negotiated, as he was able to get the hotel in 1969 (deeded June 27, 1969) for a 1958 price. LaForge had bought out his partner in 1966.

Charles LaForge, the longest tenured innkeeper ever at the Beekman Arms, circa 1980s. Here he poses in the "Pewter Room" for a sugar advertisement. LaForge was always very engaging and was a fixture in the community, the way innkeepers used to be. *Photo courtesy of Charles LaForge.*

LaForge and his first wife, Sue Bebo (another Cornell Hotel School grad), mortgaged the hotel for $250,000, paying $125,000 for the hotel and putting the other $125,000 into renovation. Floors were stripped, paint was applied, individual bathrooms were installed in the upper floors and new furnishings were added to every room. The attic contained the former servant quarters and was kept as-is and used as storage.

Through his long tenure, LaForge brought to the old hotel a significant amount of positive change. He immediately moved the main entrance and hotel desk from the north room to the main lobby (likely the first landlord ever to do so since Potter/Jacques). He expanded the north rear dining area and added public toilets and a coatroom. He also added the "wine cellar dining area" to the south side of the bar. In 1971, he acquired the adjacent firehouse building, turning it into retail space. In the late 1970s, he enlarged the kitchen, doubling its size by adding a bakeshop, prep area, walk-in cooler, storage area and office for the chef. In 1975, he bought the old laundromat property behind the inn and turned that into guest rooms. He renovated the barn and turned that into an antique shop. He acquired and renovated the circa 1844 Delamater House just up the Post Road. He also bought and then moved the antique Germond House from just south of the BA (where the bank was expanding) to a location just behind the Delamater House. In total, he eventually added forty-three rooms to his inventory.[160]

In January 1982, LaForge finished his most controversial change, adding a large "greenhouse" to the front of the south wing. At first rejected by townsfolk as an architectural abomination, it soon became the most sought-after dining space in the entire restaurant area. It also provided much-needed seating in the main function room. In 1995, he commenced another major restoration of the BA. He refreshed all the rooms, replaced wiring, updated bathrooms, replaced furniture and installed a badly needed fire sprinkler system. (The hotel suffered several chimney fires from guests throwing items into the open fireplaces and a few kitchen fires, but nothing serious. The only notable fire was in 1964, when there was a small attic fire over the rear kitchen. It caused upward of $15,000 in damages.) LaForge considered building a ratskeller in the basement, but that never came to be. An archaeological dig he sponsored under the bar room floor in 1974 yielded a handful of small old artifacts such as arrowheads and buttons.[161]

LaForge also held other hotel interests. He established "Wayfarer Inns, Inc." in 1958. His business model (with Fahey until 1966) was to lease/own and operate old colonial inns. He operated the Crane Inn in Dalton, Massachusetts; the Poughkeepsie Inn; the Governor Clinton Hotel in Kingston, New York; the Skyline Inn in Manchester, Vermont; the Johnston Inn in Johnston, New York; the Fort William Henry Hotel at Lake George; the Westport Inn and Country Club, on Lake Champlain; and the Danbury Inn in Danbury, Connecticut. In the early years, LaForge relied on assistant managers to run the BA on a day-to-day basis. Over time, the Beekman Arms became his pride and joy, so these other interests were eventually sold or discontinued. LaForge's time was also taken up by being a board member of the Culinary Institute of America and the New York State Hotel Association.

Civically in town, LaForge naturally assumed the role of innkeeper of old. He was on countless town committees, including one in the early 1970s to restore the village area and keep its appearance in "turn-of-the-century"

This is a 1973 view. The Beekman coat-of-arms is lost by now, but 1700 remains on the sign. The 1982 greenhouse had yet to be added; a maroon canvas awning served to protect patrons from the sun and rain. Duncan Hines gave the hotel a good travel recommendation. *Courtesy of the BA.*

Rear barn in spring 2013. It was destroyed by fire in 1902 and immediately rebuilt. It was used by Mr. Foster to stable horses and give lessons. Foster's love of horses led him to decorate his circa 1933 Foster's Coach House restaurant just up the street with an equestrian theme. The BA barn has served as an antique shop since the LaForge era. A photo from 1938 shows windows in the front.

style. He offered free BA space to an untold number of business and civic meetings, and he sponsored scholarships, golf tournaments and sports teams. When asked, he stepped up and began catering events at the fairgrounds, such as for IBM Family Day and the Northeast Craft Fair.

In 1975, LaForge and a group of businessmen paid off the mortgage on the old Lloyd Chrysler dealership property on East Market Street (where the doughboy statue is presently located) and converted it into much-needed parking. Collectively, they donated it to the town. In 1959, the Dutch Arms Fife and Drum Corp was organized by former town historian Dewitt Gurnell, reestablishing the age-old musical tradition in town. The band frequently played on the hotel's front lawn, adding much to the BA's colonial charm (the group disbanded sometime in the early 1980s). In 1975–76, LaForge hosted many of the bicentennial events in town.[162]

In 1980, Sue passed away after a year-long battle with cancer. Their daughter, Suzanne, attended Cornell's hotel school like her parents and married another hotel school graduate, but they both moved out of the industry. During the last ten years of his tenure starting in 1991, LaForge leased out the hotel's bar and restaurant business to notable New York City chef Larry Forgione. Larry named it the Beekman 1766 Tavern and the restaurant apparently went on to get a number of rave reviews.[163] This arrangement gave LaForge and his second wife, Ann, more time to travel, pursue golf and find their retirement home on the east coast of Florida. (Ann played a significant role at the inn herself, serving as business manager and accountant.)

LaForge held the old hotel touching six decades, from the late 1950s through to the early 2000s. A significant amount of change occurred through this long era. The Kingston Bridge's opening in 1957 changed traffic patterns. The establishment of the Culinary Institute of America in 1972 changed the restaurant landscape with the new waves of chefs it brought to the area. Cole Palen's Old Rhinebeck Aerodrome came in 1960, increasing tourism. The sloop *Clearwater* (launched in 1969) and environmental movement came, as did other influences such as fast food, the bicentennial, disco, the moon landings, MLK, JFK, Japanese cars, Vietnam, the Cold War, Watergate, the oil embargo and Iranian crisis, Munich, the 747, AIDS, the end of apartheid, the collapse of the Soviet Union, the first Gulf War, September 11, color TV, VCRs, the pocket calculator, the microprocessor and the Internet, cellphones, IBM expanding and then contracting and a million other life events. All of these impacted the Beekman Arms and the citizens of Rhinebeck during his long tenure.

Through all this, remarkably, the Beekman Arms did not change much at all. It remained a stalwart emblem of home and stability.

The list of famous celebrities who have visited is endless, from Paul Newman and Elizabeth Taylor to Nelson Rockefeller, Neil Armstrong, Billy Joel, Tip O'Neill and many, many others. In the 1960s and early '70s, LaForge also hosted and was famous for the much anticipated "Ankony Cattle Pre-sale Party." It was one of the biggest and most lively events of the year, attended by up to 350 guests. LaForge owned and ran the BA for forty-four years, longer than any other innkeeper. Both his well-timed parsimoniousness and generosity helped him succeed. When asked if he missed anything since he sold the BA in 2002, his simple response was "pride of ownership."

George Banta, successful restaurateur in the Hudson Valley area and Cornell alum, once told Chuck that he should give him a call if he was ever interested in selling the Beekman Arms. In 2002, knowing his daughter Suzanne did not want the business, LaForge eventually called George, and the reins were passed.

CHAPTER 14

The Banta Family

W hen George and Phebe (Townsend) Banta of Poughkeepsie received the phone call from Chuck LaForge, they were ecstatic and knew they were lucky. A previous deal to sell it to someone associated with the restaurant side of the Beekman Arms had just fallen through. On September 19, 2002, they bought the BA and Delamater House.[164] The Beekman Arms is the crown jewel in the Banta's portfolio of restaurants and hotels. In addition to the BA, they also own the Rhinebeck Village Inn just south of the village, three guesthouses in town, and they have investments in several local restaurants. In total, they offer ninety guest rooms in the village and are the largest hoteliers in the region (they also own twenty Super 8 Hotels, several Howard Johnson and Holiday Inn Express motels and the local Uno Chicago Grill and Buffalo Wild Wing chains). Those living in the region may remember their signature restaurant down in Wappinger Falls, Banta's Steak and Stein. Although they have a large portfolio to manage, they have an office in the BA and try to come to Rhinebeck weekly. They employ over one hundred people in Rhinebeck alone.

The Dutch heritage of the area and of the Beekman Arms is among the reasons why George was especially interested in acquiring this property. George is a member of the Holland Society. Eligibility to join comes from documented descendancy of a male family member who lived here under Dutch rule before 1675, and Banta is one of the oldest Dutch family names in New York. The flags he often has flown at the inn are meant to pay homage to the original settlers of the region (Dutch, German, British, Canadian and French).

The Banta family on September 19, 2002, the day they bought the BA and Delamater properties. Shown are daughter Jane, George, Phebe, son George Jr. (another Cornell grad) and son-in-law Richard Fisher holding grandson and future Beekman Arms landlord Richard Jr. The year 2014 celebrates fifty-five years of Cornell Hotel School–educated management at the BA. *Courtesy of the BA.*

While the Bantas have been making much-needed investments in routine maintenance, they have also added elsewhere to the property. In 2003, they built the Townsend House, connecting the BA to the old firehouse (which also remained part of the property). The Townsend House contains the four most elegant rooms of the inn. In 2012, they completely renovated the entire south wing ball room. The Bantas are also very proud of their transformation of the front lawn into a manicured garden for the village to enjoy. One of their future plans is to remove the greenhouse, a feature they do not believe fits the inn, and turn it into a covered outdoor patio area that can be enclosed European-style with sliding walls during the winter.

In 2008, a group of townspeople along with artist Jeanne Fleming brought back the "Sinterklaas Festival" to Rhinebeck after a long hiatus. This annual festival celebrates the town's Dutch roots with a grand performance of St. Nicholas arriving on his horse. Two weekends of holiday merrymaking with music, arts, crafts and an evening parade follows. During this event, the Bantas open the Beekman Arms up on the inside and outside for all visitors to enjoy. The south wing becomes one of the event's largest stages.

Rhinebeck celebrates its Dutch heritage annually with the welcoming of Sinterklaas. This two-weekend festival attracts musicians, artists and thousands of well-wishers who watch and participate in the parades, shows and other festivities. The BA is to the left. *2012 photo courtesy of Douglas Baz.*

Connected to the rear of the BA is the 2003 Townsend House. It contains the inn's four finest rooms. To the right is the circa 1870 firehouse purchased by Chuck LaForge in 1971. The upstairs now contains rooms for the BA. The downstairs storefronts contain a chocolate and gift store. A wedding carriage passes it in this August 24, 2013 photo.

Henry Delamater House on Montgomery Street. Designed by Alexander Jackson Davis in the "American Carpenter Gothic" style for Henry Delamater (local merchant at White Corner, bank president and, interestingly, one-time part owner of the BA). It was acquired by Chuck LaForge with a partner and sold with the BA to the Bantas. It operates both as a B&B and a conference center. The Bantas also own both properties adjacent to this one. *Library of Congress HABS photo, possibly 1933.*

One of the more noteworthy recent events occurred in July 2010, when Chelsea Clinton married Marc Mezvinsky at nearby Astor Courts. The town was overwhelmed with sightseers and well-wishers, but the event turned out to be a huge success. President and Mrs. Clinton hosted an after-dinner party at the Beekman Arms and also stopped by for lunch one day. A table in the rear dining room where the Clintons sat and dined now has a small metal plaque above it labeling it as the Clinton table.

The Bantas came into ownership when the world as we had known it was drastically changing. The country was still recoiling from the terrorist attacks of September 11, 2011, and it had just begun ideological wars in Afghanistan in 2001 and Iraq in 2003. Deceit and corruption had taken down high-flying companies such as Enron and WorldCom. Church abuses were being exposed. The Internet was opening the world's eyes to massive issues in labor exploitation and human rights abuses. Everyone in this country, it seemed, was reexamining priorities and becoming much more pragmatic in their ways. This certainly impacted the hospitality industry. Fortunately, positive influences were taking greater hold. The Internet and "ecommerce" would explode with new innovation. "Google" and "social media" would become much-used phrases in our collective vocabulary. Mainstream media would be replaced with more powerful means to communicate and spread news. The nation's leadership would change parties and attempt to chart a new direction for the country. Corporate social responsibility would be a force for change. GPS and digital mapping systems would change how we travel and view the world. Wind, solar and shale gas would begin powering the country and doing less harm to the climate. The challenges of AIDS would be met, and the human genome would be mapped. LED and battery technology would change entertainment viewing and telecommunications. Through all this, the BA continued on, not failing to be reshaped by this innovation.

The Bantas are long-term owners, and at least two generations of children and grandchildren are destined to remain in the business. As it always has, the BA will continue to evolve to meet the needs of the community. It is good to know it is in the hands of a family with the financial means, skills, generosity and foresight to keep it running properly.

CHAPTER 15

Layout and Inside Descriptions

The Beekman Arms is a relatively simple structure. As one enters the main lobby, to the left is a small dining room known as the Pewter Room. It seems to have served this function for a long time. In ye old days, it quite possibly could have been dedicated family space. The main lobby seems to have always been the living/sitting room. A less formal bar/saloon appears to have been in the north wing (at least from 1886 to 1912, according to the Sanborn maps.) The north wing entrance was historically the inn's main entrance, as it was convenient to the stage running to and from the river. In the early 1900s, the north wing appears to include a soda fountain and possibly a cigar store. In the early 1800s, it was a drygoods store. After Prohibition was repealed in 1933, Winne and Dows added a large brick kitchen behind the building in 1935 and turned the kitchen in the hotel's rear into the taproom. (Also in the Winne era, south of the hotel across the drive was a tea garden. Winne advertised: "In its cozy nooks and corners enclosed by rows of stately cedars and hedges, banked with shrubbery and flowering plants, one [found] comfortable chairs for a quiet afternoon tea.")

When LaForge came, he made the layout changes we see today. For the first time since the Jacques era, the front desk was moved into the main lobby. His changes in the kitchen were less noticable, except as seen in improved service. During the 1990s, when the restaurant function was leased out, a high-end food store was for a brief time in part of the north wing. Today, the north wing is a library/sitting room along with additional dining space. The BA has twenty-three guest rooms, including four in the Townsend house, two

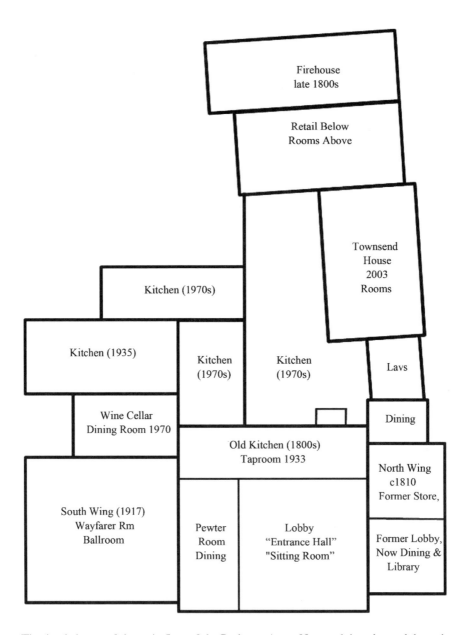

The simple layout of the main floor of the Beekman Arms. Not much has changed through the years. The lobby in the circa 1805 north wing moved to the entrance hall in the early 1960s. The south wing was added in 1917. What is now the tap room historically had been the kitchen. *Map/Imagedata: ©2013 Google, DigitalGlobe.*

in the firehouse and four in the detached rear guesthouse. Thirteen rooms are in the original structure, with four rooms in the 1917 wing, six rooms on the third floor and three rooms on the second floor (hotel offices also fill this second-floor space).

Others through the ages provide some insight on how the hotel/inn functioned:

LAYOUT (LAKE, 1894)

The *Poughkeepsie Daily Eagle* on April 11, 1894, noted that "Mr. V.D. Lake, the new proprietor of the Rhinebeck Hotel, has refurnished the hotel and made some important changes; one of which is that the dining room which has been in the rear of the house for years, is now located in the front, south room, which is much more desirable."

LAYOUT (WELLES, 1907)

Halleck Welles seems to be the first person who sensed the possible historical significance of the old hotel. Prior to this, it seems the old hotel was just a typical functional business of the day, trying to stay "modern." A May 11, 1907 *Rhinebeck Gazette* article, described the remodeling done by Welles:

NOVEL ROOM AT THE HOTEL

With "the hanging of the crane" the redecoration and transformation of the sitting room of the Rhinebeck Hotel was completed. When Mr. Welles delved into the past of the house on taking charge last Fall he learned of its exceptional age and historical interest. He conceived the idea of making one room correspond with the most eventful period of its existence and secured the services of W.F. Weckesser of this village to aid in producing what is now one of the "show places" along the old Post Road. The room briefly described shows the age stained ceiling of smooth and polished planks supported by beams 6x8 inches placed 4 feet apart. The walls are calcimined a soft dull yellow showing complete harmony with the old mahogany wainscoting veneer beneath. Several ancient prints hang on the wall and also an engraved portrait of General John Armstrong who was a guest at the hotel until his death in 1843. Another picture of Washington and his generals, all portraits, is very interesting. Another of the barque Oscar of Sag Harbor, L.I., on which a mutiny is in progress, defies all laws of perspective. Mahogany framed mirrors, swords, flint locks and lanterns fill up all other spaces. A plate board crosses two sides of the room on which rest dishes of all shapes and colors, memories of the past, some of them have served in the hotel longer than the "oldest inhabitant" has lived, others have done duty on the tables of the oldest families of this country while others are heirlooms in Mr. Welle's family which dates back on Long Island to 1640. The larger cabinets filling one whole side of the room are filled with attractive and curious pieces of brass, pewter and china, chief of which is the "Big Blue Pitcher." The fire place is a conspicuous feature. The mantel is pure white, of simple colonial design. It was the property in 1798, of Janet Montgomery, widow of General Richard Montgomery. Imported blue and white tiles frame the opening in which swings the crane and kettle of copper over brass andirons and tiles of red making a picture of simplicity and comfort. Nearby stand a flax wheel with its curious spinning light, a foot stove, a brass bed warming pan, an antique work box and the tongs and shovel so necessary to the management of an open fire. The big clock in a corner close by ticks in a dignified, contented way as it has done for nearly two centuries. A fine old table fills the center of the room and clustered around it are delicate high backed mesh bottomed spindle chairs long used in the Wynkoop family. Other easy chairs, quaint tables, an inviting hair cloth sofa and rag carpet rugs galore complete the furnishing and form a picture of the restful old time days when peace and plenty filled the land after the Revolution.

Mr. Weckesser has added anew to his reputation as a decorator of true artistic sense while Ackert & Brown, Augustas Van Keuren and John Milroy who fashioned the wood work, framed the fire place and shaped the crane have left nothing to be desired in their respective lines. The room was conceived and executed in Rhinebeck without a suggestion from book or person outside and its counterpart does not exist from "Dan to Beersheba."

LAYOUT (WELLES, 1907)

Later in 1907, Welles produced his *Reminiscences of the Oldest Hotel in America* booklet. Without knowing Welles made all of these changes with the help of an interior decorator, one would think he was describing an old tavern room that had always been there. Welles probably used some imagination when he wrote:

Traphagen built a one-story stone house of two rooms with a loft above. The kitchen, which still is used as such, was then the general living room while the other and larger apartment served as the public room. A little bar in one corner, a big fireplace with rude benches in front of it offered travelers of those days comforts not always met with in a day's journey. A pile of sheep skins formed his bed before the fire while the family climbed to the loft for sleep…The general arrangement of the rooms and walls of the older part remain the same. The dining room is the same that all the guests of the past, great and humble, have broken fast. The fireplace there is the same before which one night in 1813 Aaron Burr and Gen'l. Armstrong sat chatting…The old tap room, in which guests of all the ages of the house have gathered, is now used as a sitting room. The huge brown beams and planks of the ceiling are there as the builders placed them. The rough walls are white washed and a plate rail extending across two sides of the room is filled with remnants of crockery and pewter used in the primitive days of the 18th and 19th centuries. Flintlocks hang on the beams and swords cross on the chimney breast and, below, the pure white mantel rises above the Dutch tiled fireplace and hearth over which hang crane and kettle. The mantel dates to 1798 and was then the property of Janet [Montgomery]…The sitting room is kept free from modern innovations and the spinning wheel, the fine old Dutch spindle chairs, the 200 years old clock ticking off correct time under wooden works, the old prints, the rare china, the rag carpets, and the many other accessories of the apartment are never profaned by the presence of things more modern than guests…The wooden wing on the north end in which the office and bar are now located was added about 1810. It was built for use as a general store.

Layout (Morse, 1908)

Morse tells readers:

In the old hotel, the taproom was in the northeast room. The bar was an enclosed nook in the corner beyond the chimney. A short counter, with grill work above, a closet and shelves behind and shelves underneath, made the bar. It was entered on the lower side; a narrow passage was left for the purpose; it had a wooden portcullis, raised or lowered as required. Quoit-pitching, running, wrestling and shooting-matches were common. The dining-room and kitchen were in the rear of the tap-room. The guest chambers on the upper floor. This portion of the "old hotel" is practically the same today, that is the old stone part, as it was when Traphagen built it.

LAYOUT (LATHROP, 1926)

Lathrop tells readers:

The old portion of the present Beekman Arms consists of the present living-room or entrance hall, into which the old hallway has been thrown, the large room on the left, and part of the present kitchen. All three rooms had old

This photograph, circa early 1900s, shows the old main lobby, which was in the north wing. Stages from the river, which likely were more frequent than those coming up the Post Road, found this entrance more convenient and the hotel just adapted to the changing needs. Note the soda counter to the left and the room's strikingly "modern" appearance (the historic décor was yet to come). *Photo courtesy of MRH.*

fireplaces. The one in the kitchen has been removed, but in a basement room beneath is an old oven which the present proprietor is somewhat at a loss to account for, since the room is only five feet high, and one can hardly imagine cooking being done where the cook could not stand erect. If the floor was raised, or the ceiling lowered, it must have been done many years ago. The right wing was added about a hundred years ago, the other by the present proprietor when he took the house twelve years ago.

A September 15, 1917 *Rhinebeck Gazette* article also describes the inside décor: "The parlor on the second floor has been made handsome and homelike with its carefully selected furnishings, the sleeping rooms are dainty and inviting with their ivory enameled furniture and delicate papering. Each room is furnished with hot and cold water, besides a bath room in close proximity." A November 21, 1931 *Rhinebeck Gazette* article mentions it had a second-floor private dining room. (Lewis Winne built this in 1930).

CHAPTER 16

Oldest in America

The small booklet written by Halleck Welles in 1907 is where the claim of "Oldest Hotel in America" first appears. It could have come before his time, but nothing has been found suggesting the claim is any older. In 1909, Arthur Shuffle broadcast the claim by hanging a sign across the Post Road. Starting in 1914, Wally Foster played up the title with the endless series of newspaper ads and postcards he produced (which Lewis Winne picked up on and continued for the next twenty years).

We see the BA on a map in 1802 labeled as a hotel, so there is some proof the business is at least 211 years old and there are no older hotels in the United States today.[165] In Halleck's days, it would have already been just over 100 years old. One would need to research all the old hotels that were still in existence back in that era to see if his original claim was even valid. There does seem to have been a few older inns around. The Ye Old Canoe Place Inn in Hampton Bays, Long Island, dated to 1657 and stood through Welles's era (it burned down in 1921). The Perkliomen Bridge Hotel, northwest of Philadelphia, closed now, claimed to date from 1706. The Elm Tree Inn in Farmington, Connecticut, another noted old historic inn, supposedly dates back to 1660. When Elise Lathrop's book *Early American Inns and Taverns* came out in 1926, Rhinebeck was a bit shocked. An August 16, 1930 *Rhinebeck Gazette* article interprets that her casual single use of the word "hotel" in her running description of the Elm Tree made it a de facto hotel in the eyes of the *Rhinebeck Gazette*, thereby making the BA the *second*-oldest hotel in America. The local information section of the

Rhinebeck Gazette still called the BA the second-oldest on February 7, 1931. Locals seemed to have changed their mind on this, perhaps sticking to the view that the Elm Tree is a tavern/inn, not a hotel. It is a moot issue now, as the building turned into condominiums long ago.

The oldest hotel in Boston, the Parker House, now the Omni Parker House, was built in 1855 and then completely demolished and rebuilt circa 1927. (The Parker House is where Parker House rolls and Boston cream pie were first created.) Boston's Union Oyster House, circa 1826, claims to be the "Oldest Restaurant in America."

New York City's oldest hotel is the Cosmopolitan Hotel, at Chambers Street and West Broadway, built in 1845. It is still in existence, but it has closed several times over the years. The Fraunces Tavern, circa 1762, is older, but it burned down several times, stopped operating and claims to be a tavern, not a hotel. Today it is an out-of-period modern restaurant with a detached upstairs museum.

Chicago's oldest hotel is the 1871 Palmer House. The DeSoto House in Galena, Illinois, still open and operating, dates to 1855 and is well known as one of the oldest. Other historic United States cities, including Philadelphia, St. Augustine and Santa Fe, have nothing older than these.

Around the bicentennial, Chuck LaForge began changing the attribution from "hotel" to the more colonial sounding "inn," and thus the dispute began on which tavern/inn was the oldest.

The debate requires one to more clearly define what is an inn, what is a tavern and what is a hotel (and whether they can change back and forth). The answer is always subjective. Inns and taverns were generally equivalent. They both typically had barns behind them to take care of "beasts" in addition to guests. Tavern fare and colonial customs seemed to be more associated with them. Both often offered lodging. Hotels had "modern" services, which likely over time included separate beds and rooms, maid service, a front desk, a fine dining room and other amenities associated with travel. If one puts the Beekman Arms in the older category of an inn/tavern, it does have some stiff competition.

The Concord Inn in Concord, Massachusetts, was built in 1716 (it claims), but the inn/hotel business did not start until 1889. The Griswold Inn in Griswold, Connecticut, circa 1776, says it is "one of the oldest continuously operated inns in the country."[166] (There is no information on how long it has actually been open.)

The White Horse Tavern in Newport, Rhode Island, has very early roots. It claims 1673, but one would need to see evidence proving the building is this old. Also, from 1895 to 1957, it did not serve as a tavern. It has no barn or overnight guest function, but it still makes the claim it is the "oldest tavern in America."

New Orleans has Lafitte's Blacksmith Shop, said to be built between 1722 and 1732 (Lafitte himself was born in 1776). It is reputed to be the oldest structure used as a bar in the United States (so not a tavern or inn at all).

Longfellow's Wayside Inn (originally known by the family name of How's Tavern) in Sudbury, Massachusetts, has the best claim. Official innkeeping records exist from 1716 in state archives. Though its long tenure was disrupted for thirty-two years when it functioned as a farmhouse, it has been continuously open as a tavern/inn since 1893 (and run as a tavern for 266 total years). It also still has a functioning barn and can "entertain" beasts, so arguably it is the only true inn/tavern left.

The Beekman Arms' claim as an inn has on and off been augmented with the specific claim of being "America's oldest *continuously operating* inn in America" (currently it claims simply to be the "Oldest Inn in America"). The "continuously operating" is a valid claim, as its 212 years with little disruption trumps the Wayside Inn's latest run of 121 years. They are both old and treasured landmarks on the American landscape, so we will leave the debate here.

CHAPTER 17

Other Early Rhinebeck Taverns

Taverns and inns played a vital role in early settlements, serving as the center for communication, travel, politics and social interaction. As a farming community with a relatively small population on fairly sizable lots, Rhinebeck was becoming quite spread out. At the same time, its docks, mills and quarries were bringing in travelers from all directions. As the needs of the people and commerce routes shifted and changed, other taverns came into existence. Most are long gone and forgotten, but in their heydays, they were indispensable parts of the community. As Morse says:

> At these taverns the hungry, thirsty and worn traveler found rest, comfort, shelter, good suppers and wine…Saturday evenings from over the town men came to the nearest tavern to hear the news. Monfort's on the south end, Marquart's in Wurtemburgh, Moul's at Kirchehoek, Kip's in Kipsbergen, the "old hotel" on the flatts, found goodly numbers discussing politics, theology and the crops; playing checkers, dominos and cards; telling stories in the capacious tap-rooms around a cheerful blazing fire on a winter's night, whiling away the time with mugs of flip and malted cider. In the days of Potter, farmers brought pork, poultry, butter, eggs, grain, and other products for him to market for them.

The Alexander Thompson maps identify all of Rhinebeck's inns (none were labeled as taverns) from 1798 to 1800. It is interesting to note that in just the two years from the first to the fourth copy, a few names had already changed, and a few taverns seemed to have come and gone. This highlights the fact that all maps, particularly those with labeled houses, are but a snapshot in time. The following is a brief inventory of inns just in present-day Rhinebeck (excluding Red Hook, which was part of Rhinebeck until 1812).

The 1798 Starr Library map (the old [Starr] "Institute" map) shows eight inns: Mowl's Inn (a few hundred feet north of where 9/9G meet, near milestone 101, still exists today as a private home); Potter's Inn; Kip's Inn (Montgomery Street near Chestnut); Eckert's Inn (near where East Market Street and South Street meet); "Inn" (at dock); Steenberg's Inn (west side of Post Road, just before the village, where it still exists as a private home); Montfoort's Inn (west side of Post Road south of village near Red Tail Road, which did not exist at that time, and the inn no longer exists. Smith adds that "Monfort's" had a doorknocker with a 1760 date on it); and Marquart's Inn on Wurtemberg Road (just south of St. Paul's Church on the west side of the road, no longer exists). All four of the Thompson maps also show a Morris's Inn farther east out near Patten Road/Lake Sepascot.[167]

The 1798 NYSA map shows six inns: Moul's Inn, Potter's Inn, Kip's Inn, Steenbergh's Inn, Monfort's Inn and Marquart's Inn. (We believe this is a cleaned up/stripped down version of the Institute map submitted to the state.)

The 1799 Montgomery Place map (now in the possession of Hudson River Heritage) shows eight inns: Mawl's Inn, Kip's Inn, Ostrander's Inn (north side of E. Market St., a few hundred feet up from town center), Eckert's Inn, Cox's Inn (at dock), Steenberg's, Montford's Inn, and Marquart's Inn. Potter's exists as "Mr. Potter," and it is not identified as a tavern.

The 1800 Library of Congress map shows seven inns: Mowl's Inn, Eckert's Inn, Cox's Inn (on or near the lot where Church of the Messiah was built in 1853), Kip's Inn, Brown's Inn (in Steenberg's place), Montfort's Inn and J. Marquart's Inn. (Potter's seems to have changed to a house.)

When these maps were being published, the stagecoach industry was just growing into its full glory. By virtue of its convenient location, Rhinebeck was an important stop, and shrewd businessmen were always looking for new opportunities here. More inns and taverns were to come. In 1802, Potter bought the old Bogardus property and established a hotel (our BA, which turned into Jacques Hotel/Stagehouse three years later). Another stagehouse/tavern, Brinckerhoff's, appears just east of the town center (possibly for a trunk line stage).

On all these other old inns and taverns, history is virtually silent. Two have just a brief few sentences on them, passed down through the ages, to give hints of their long but lost tales—Brinckerhoff's (later known as Pultz's Tavern, then as the Bowery), and one called Tammany Hall.

The Bowery was built circa 1800 by Abrams Brinckerhoff as a stagecoach house.[168] It was located on East Market Street, two lots east of the present Catholic church (a New York State historical sign marks its location). Large barns were in its yard. Morse tells us that since this was (RDC) church property, it had to get a formal release to sell liquor (which he says it did on September 2, 1801). He adds:

> *Peter Pultz, a respected citizen, succeeded Brinckerhoff. Pultz's tavern became a town institution, rivaling the "old hotel." It had its own clientele. The "Yellow Bird" stage line quartered there. No pains were spared to attract custom[ers]…Novelty in entertainment or instruction was one of the variety of uses to which the Pultz tavern was put from its earliest days. Within its walls there was a constant moving panorama; before its doors distinguished, picturesque and unwonted guests passed and repassed. For those on duty or pleasure bent it was a gathering place. It was the centre of life and affairs for a large section…Its popularity waned after the retirement of Mr. Pultz, because of old age. It was given the name of the "Bowery House," and is still standing, but no longer a tavern.*

By 1859, the Bowery was owned by Rowland Marquet (while at the same time Martin Marquart owned the BA. It is not known if there was a connection). By 1894, the Bowery was the "City Laundry" and the April 21, 1894 *Rhinebeck Gazette* notes it was "being painted and partially repaired." By 1895, it was a dwelling (shown on the Sanborn maps). By 1960, it was gone. An October 27, 1960 *Rhinebeck Gazette* article notes that it suffered a devastating fire that left it a total loss.

Tammany Hall was located on Montgomery Street, almost opposite of Ruge's Garage.[169] The name was a contemporary name for one of the older taverns on this site, Kip's Tavern. There is little doubt the name derived from the powerful New York City "Anti-Federalist" political society (the early Democrats) and their headquarters of the same name, but not much is known about this old Rhinebeck tavern. Smith provides a listing of the "old 'Tammany Hall' hotel stand" ownership dating back to 1746 (apparently it was a tavern since at least 1762). It was owned by a gunsmith from 1769 to 1783, so presumably it was not a tavern when Erskine came through in 1779.

As he did for the BA, Morse gives Tammany Hall all kinds of character (writing one hundred years after its days as a tavern). He follows Smith's

Ads for the Bowery Hotel, which was located on East Market Street near the center of the village. Found in the March 3, 1863, and March 26, 1861 editions of the *Rhinebeck Gazette*. *Courtesy of the RHS.*

ownership progression of how it got passed along, eventually to John A. Kips by 1798. In 1804, the "heated" gubernatorial political match between General Morgan Lewis and Aaron Burr was said to have occurred. Morse tells us this tavern was Burr's headquarters, and the BA was Lewis's, although no mention is made of this in Burr's memoirs or in any newspapers found.[170] Morse also provides a rough sense of its location, placing it "above what is now Chestnut Street."[171]

Both Smith and Morse likely had access to the Institute map and the circa 1798 John Cox map and relied on them.[172] Both maps show the Kip and Potter taverns. The Cox map actually shows their labeled plot locations. Using the scale provided, Kip's clearly is near Chestnut Street, and Potter's seems to be on the west side of Montgomery Street, just across the street and a few feet north of Platt Avenue. Smith confirms this inn, stating, "Asa Potter, who, according to the Institute map, was an inn keeper in a house in the vicinity of the present residence of Mrs. W. B. Platt." This location of Potter's seems to be where Trimper's tavern/brewhouse was located.

Kip's/Tammany's location is further validated by the oral history. A February 22, 1919 *Rhinebeck Gazette* article says, "Old Tammany passed into the hands of the Schryver family." The article has an interview with "MVB Schryver" in which he states his grandfather and father lived there. The Schryvers' lot just north of Chestnut Street can be seen on the 1867 Beer's map (it is where the car lot is today, across from Ruge's Service Station). Similarly, a 1920 DAR photo of a building on this site labels it as Tammany Hall. Kips/Tammany was on this site at least until July 28, 1966, when town

In 1918, Tracy Dows hired Harry Coutant to photograph all the old structures in town. He captured these four old taverns. Clockwise from top left: Tammany Hall, where Ruge's Subaru showroom now stands on west side of Montgomery Street, razed sometime after 1966; Moul's Inn, still in existence near the 9/9G intersection; Steenberg's Inn, still in existence as a home, west side of Post Road before the village; and the Bowery, East Market Street, destroyed by fire in 1960. *All photos now in the DAR Collection and used courtesy of the RHS.*

historian Dewitt Gurnell wrote about it in the *Rhinebeck Gazette*. He cites the Tammany Hall history word for word from Morse but notes the building is for sale and it would be nice to preserve it as a museum. It is unclear when it was pulled down, but when Ruge's new car showroom was built in 2001, the spot had been a vacant lot for many years already. The small barn on the site is very old, and it was restored.

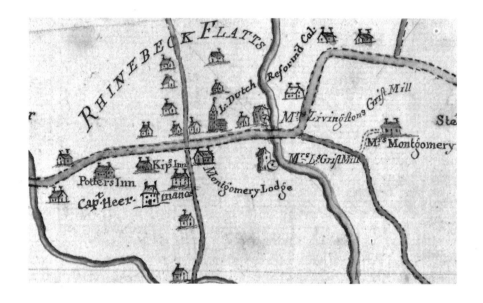

Excerpt from "Map of the Town of Rhinebeck, In the County of Dutches~, Surveyed in Dec & Jan 1797 and 1798, per Alexr Thompson." One of four copies of this map. There is no mention of Bogardus, and "Montgomery Lodge" is a prominent label for the BA. *Courtesy of the New York State Archives.*

Conclusion

A nation must believe in three things. It must believe in the past. It must believe in the future. It must, above all, believe in the capacity of its own people so to learn from the past that they can gain in judgment in creating their own future.
—FDR, at his library dedication, June 30, 1941

So now we leave the Old Albany Post Road and the Beekman Arms, ninety-eight miles and once four days from New York City. It was because of the early Beekman and Traphagen families that the village of Rhinebeck came to be. Building and road construction, land exchanges, marriages and mobility later shaped and changed Rhinebeck. Where once two-foot paths crossed in the wilderness, a busy and lively intersection now exists.

Standing at this street corner today, perhaps in the same spot where our forefathers once stood, both residents and visitors alike can see and sense the rich history all about. Many have heard the story. Morse and Smith have served admirably over the past one hundred years to provide some of it. Now there is just more to add. New data and new analysis tools, as well as our generation's less-innocent proclivity to question everything written or told to us, combine to bring more rigor and refinement into our examination of the past. The facts we found took us in a surprisingly different direction than what was anticipated when we started this book. Rather than the story of an old colonial tavern steeped in traditions and tavern lore, the Beekman Arms' story seems to be one of an early mercantile and trading business that profited from its ideal location at the crossroad. As the needs of the community—and the landlords—changed, it adapted and became one of the most noted stagecoach houses on the circuit to Albany. Almost a century ago now, visionaries transformed it into the grand historic structure that speaks to us today.

Through all the changes in Rhinebeck, from agriculture to tourism, from the grand estates to their repurposed non-profit uses, from slate to violets, from horse to horseless, from gristmills to supermarkets, from the ferry to bridge, one thing has remained constant: the Beekman Arms, in whatever form or name it took, has always stood in the center. It is a cherished reminder of our Dutch and English heritage, and it is what helps makes Rhinebeck a community like no other in the Hudson Valley.

As we look back on our quest to bring you this story, we are reminded of what Plato wrote long ago: "As it is the commendation of a good huntsman to find game in a wide wood, so it is no imputation if he has not caught all." There is undoubtedly more information on the Beekman Arms hidden away somewhere, awaiting future discovery. If we were successful at least in keeping some of Rhinebeck's history from slipping into the shadows and if we have opened the door for others to look for more on the town's history, then we have done, with great pleasure, what we set out to do.

$\mathcal{Notes}$

PREFACE

1. The opening quote is an excerpt of a poem by A. Allen titled "A New-Hampshire Tavern." It can be found in Dunbar, *History of Travel in America*, 1:213. It was originally published in the 1821 *New England Almanack*.

2. This date and the Warren's Tavern reference are provided in the *Putnam County Republican* on August 22, 1940, page 1, and also in Eberlin's *Historic Houses of the Hudson Valley*. Anything about this old tavern requires research and verification. Warren's does not appear on early maps or in Pelletreau's *History of Putnam County*. The oldest tavern in that area was John Roger's, located a mile before this one. The tavern is currently called the Bird and Bottle Inn, a name it was given in 1940 when it was first renovated. It had until recently operated as a restaurant and country inn, but it is currently closed and looking for new ownership. With regards to the "Old" Post Road, there is nothing special about the name. There are a number of "Old Albany Post Roads" scattered throughout its length due to the various reroutes.

3. Fort Crailo, in today's Rensselaer (called Greenbush until 1897), right across the Hudson from Albany. "Crawlew" (called Crawlier by 1905) is what it was called in the original transcription of the act.

4. It has been long accepted that that Dutch built a road circa 1650 called the "Old Mine Road" (now Route 209) from Esopus (Kingston) to the

Delaware River for mining purposes. It was routed over ancient native paths. The mining use has come into question; nevertheless, the road/native paths followed for a good length the Esopus and Rondout Creeks. From the Esopus Creek near Kingston, the trail would have left the creek and come overland two miles through Kingston to the Hudson shore. At this Esopus junction, another trail, now known as the Onteora Trail, took off and headed north. Heading east, these combined trails likely would have crossed over the Hudson at Kingston Point (at the mouth of the Rondout Creek), which was the Hudson's narrowest stretch in this area. The landing point on the east side of the Hudson was a point once called Radcliffe's Landing and later referred to as Long Dock (though some argue it was at Sleight Dock). This path became Rhinecliff Road and West and East Market Streets in the Village of Rhinebeck. East of the Post Road, the trail is said to have passed a native village on Sepasco Lake. Near here is an old cave known as Welch's Cave (now a protected heritage site).

5. The Rhinebeck Historical Society remarkably has issue 1, volume 1 and a large collection of other actual papers (though it is far from being a complete collection). It also has a microfilm archive. Other archived papers are found all over, from the state archives in Albany, to the New York Historical Society, to the American Antiquarian Society, to the Adriance Library, to Fultonhistory.com, which posts hundreds of somewhat searchable separate microfilm pages.

6. State of New York, *The Colonial Laws of New York*, 1:39, "The Duke of York's Laws 1665–1675." See also *Colonial Laws of New York*, 4:729 (1763, regulate number of Dutchess Co. taverns), and 5:583 (1773, regulate taverns).

7. Item #157 in the Town Historian's Archives (kept with the RHS collection). The lead record description is "1857 Tavern Applications Signatures of Petition to Operate."

INTRODUCTION

8. A 1606 charter from King James gave the Plymouth Company the rights to land between the thirty-eight and forty-fifth parallels. By 1620, another charter from King James allotted the lands between the fortieth and forty-eighth parallels to a new group, the Plymouth Council, formed from the remnants of the Plymouth Company; this parcel of land was

termed "New England" and stretched from Philadelphia to beyond the Canadian border. It was with this new group that the Merchant Adventurers (the financial sponsors) negotiated for the pilgrims' land patents in the new world. Initially, the pilgrims were supposed to settle at the mouth of the Hudson, but they first sighted land at Cape Cod, and their efforts to sail south to the Hudson were repulsed by bad weather and treacherous currents.

9. Before the English came, the Dutch were involved in a number of conflicts with the natives. The most notable was Kieft's War (1643–45) in the area of New York City.

10. When the British took control, land settlement began to assume more of the characteristics of the feudal English manor system, with the estate's owner signified as a "lord" whose tenants were legally obligated to provide service, produce or money in exchange for their land lease. (Nine significant manors were established in New York along with seven lesser ones.) Giving away large tracts of land and setting up small empires was unacceptable to many, including the local government and the King's own advisors. Patents were also issued in the late seventeenth/ early eighteenth century. There were large land grants that did not carry the manorial system with them. Patents usually employed the use of quitrent (land use taxes) and leases. By 1895, there were 226 New York patents, tracts, reservations and manors splitting up almost the entire state of New York. See the "Map of the State of New York showing the location of the original Land Grants Patents and Purchases," 1895, by Joseph R. Bien (found in the David Rumsey map collection), for a map and list of all patents. This patent system was unique in early colonial America, where land was usually sold outright to potential owners. Ownership customs in New York gradually shifted as tenants obtained life-leases or became freeholders and began to exercise their right to vote in provincial assemblies. All land grants in New York required a prior financial settlement with the natives, although this stipulation was often ignored or led to a deceptive transaction. Beekman's March 27, 1703, Indian deed is in the Princeton Library Collection, Box 158.

11. There is no specific language requiring settlement in the Beekman patent agreement (provided on page 412 of Morse, *Historic Old Rhinebeck Echos*). There did seem to be an expectation. See McDermott, *Colonial Land Grants in Dutchess County, NY,* 1. He writes that the British Board of Trade in 1732

was very critical of the land grant system and cites from a document that "the board threatened forfeiture of land grants which did not 'plant, Settle, and effectually Cultivate, at least three Acres of Land for every fifty acres, within three years, after the same shall be granted.'"

12. Ulster County Registry of Deeds, Book AA, page 345. It seems that this description should say 21 degrees, 45 minutes. Either it was incorrect as surveyed or written, or it was later resurveyed/changed. The 1746 and 1769 plots/maps show the border on the 21 degree, 45 minute line (approximately the back of the lot lines on Oak Street).

13. At his age, he probably was well set in life over in Kingston. Becoming a pioneer and starting all over again was certainly possible, but it seems like a lot to ask. Interestingly, page 36 of the Dutchess County Yearbook for 1918 has a brief article about some of the mills in Dutchess County. On the mill in Salt Point, the author writes: "An old inhabitant stated the initials of the man who built the first mill at Salt Point are on the stone on top of the dam, and those correspond with these of Wm. Traphagen, it is fair to suppose that he was the artisan." Research is probably not possible on this claim. Who knows—maybe Traphagen was a "consultant" designing and building mills all over.

14. Deed from Elisha Potter to Richard Schell, book 62, page 604, DCRD.

15. A *Rhinebeck Gazette* article dated February 24, 1917, mentions a February 10 *Hotel Review Magazine* article that calls the BA "the Hotel American in Rhinebeck." This might be the selected, then discarded, original name (or just a simple misprint).

16. By the 1970s, this seems to have gotten lost in thought. Other colonial-looking—but inaccurate—signs not carrying the Beekman coat of arms would go up. The Beekman coat of arms incorporates the saying "*mens conscia recti*" ("their knowledge of right").

17. *The Colonial Laws of New York*, 4:720. The mid-1800 local tavern licenses on file with the town similarly do not differentiate between inn, tavern or even hotel.

18. Lathrop, *Early American Inns and Taverns,* viii. She researched dozens of these old taverns and gained significant expertise in the field. Empirical evidence can also be gathered from Bayles, *Old Taverns of New York*. "Tavern" seems to be the principal term used in New York City.

19. *Colonial Laws of New York*, 5:583.

20. Holmes and Rohrbach, *Stagecoach East*, 161.

Chapter 1

21. Dates used are the most generally accepted dates found (the historical record is filled with inconsistencies).
22. He also held the military rank of colonel (in the militia, per Smith), but his son was better known as Colonel Beekman. The original Indian deed dated March 27, 1703, in the Princeton archives, Box 158, refers to Judge Beekman as colonel, as does the 1769 map.
23. The 1710 transaction for mill property discussed in Smith, *History of Rhinebeck*, 14 is actually between Arie Roosa and Henry Beekman Jr. The deed Smith cites outlines six acres of land sold by Roosa to Beekman Jr., which skirts the mill dam already built and in the possession of Henry Beekman Sr. Smith then infers this as evidence that a gristmill and sawmill would have been in existence by this time, accessible to communities on both sides of the river, and thus probably featuring a boat dock. There is a famous 1844 Thomas Cole painting titled *Old Mill at Sunset*, which looks strikingly similar, conceptually, to a mill put on this location (albeit with the Catskills in the background moved in a little closer).
24. Edward Livingston Papers, Princeton Library, Folder 10, Box 128. Beekman list of deeds at time of his death.
25. Hasbrouck, *History of Dutchess County*, 81.
26. Blanchard, *History of the Reformed Dutch Church*, 23. Blanchard mentions the legend that Henry Beekman Jr. is buried under the pulpit. He cites an 1899 document in the "New York Historical Collections" that mentions he is buried "in" the church. The 150th anniversary book written by Drury in 1881 makes no mention of it. In 1939 as part of the post office dedication, dignitaries walked across the street to the church and had a remembrance ceremony at his grave before going inside to listen to a DAR speech. It is not clear to anyone where or what they looked at. The RDC and local historian do not know where Colonel Beekman is buried.
27. Of Robert, Margaret's father: "An ardent defender of colonists' rights, it is said that he became so agitated by the news of the battles of Lexington and Concord that he suffered a fatal heart attack." See http://www.clermontny.org/the-clermont-estate.
28. See Smith, *History of Rhinebeck*, 62. It was named "Rhinebeck House" when Janet Montgomery built and owned it, but it possibly changed to Grasmere when Peter rebuilt the mansion after it burned down in 1828.
29. Drury, *Reformed (Dutch) Church of Rhinebeck*, 24. The basis of this brief sibling description comes from this source.

Chapter 2

30. Letter from John Adams to Abigail Adams, January 19, 1777. Adams Family Papers: An Electronic Archive, Massachusetts Historical Society, http://www.masshist.org/digitaladams/.

31. Hawthorne, *Snow-Image*, 68.

32. Floyd-Jones, *Relic of the Highway*, 236.

33. After the Revolution, McGowan's (or McGown's) turned into Leggett's Tavern (which is what Colles shows in *A Survey of the Roads of the United States of America*).

34. Stephen Jenkins's book, *The Greatest Street in the World*, has a photo of a later version of this bridge. This section of the creek was dredged and rerouted, isolating a portion of Manhattan off the island (Marble Hill, which still exists).

35. Scharf, *History of Westchester County*, 749.

36. State of New York, *The Colonial Laws of New York*, 1:532. A later act passed in 1896 (State of New York, *Laws of the State of New York Passed at 119th Session of the Legislature*, 1:386) entitled "An act to preserve forever the New York and Albany post road as a State public highway" protects the highway from encroachment by the railroads and other significant changes. The 1703 act was revised several times, including in 1728, 1737 and likely other years.

37. There is no current map reference to a Clay Hill, but most likely it is near the hilly area after South Mill Street branches off from the Post Road. Morse is likely speculating with this assertion.

38. *Colonial Laws of New York*, "The Highway Act of October 30, 1708," 1:632.

39. Floyd-Jones, *Relic of the Highway*, 239.

40. Ibid., 240. He cites State of New York, *Laws of the State of New York, Comprising the Constitution, and the Acts of the Legislature, since the Revolution, from the First to the Twentieth Session, Inclusive*, 3:415.

41. State of New York, *Colonial Laws of New York*, 5:646. "An Act to prevent the breaking or defacing the Mile Stones now or hereafter to be erected in this Colony." Passed March 9, 1774. It was revised March 20, 1788. See Floyd-Jones, *Relic of the Highway*, 220. In 1797, it seems to have been revised to ten dollars (Floyd-Jones, *Relic of the Highway*, 240).

42. Marist College Archives and Special Collections department has the circa 1980 research done by Mr. and Mrs. James Spratt on the topic. There is no evidence that Ben Franklin as postmaster had anything specific to do with the milestones along the Albany Post Road.

43. Survey for Simon Cole of rhombus-shaped plot dated March 27, 1770, Princeton University Library, Box 157. Maps used were in oversize box 163. Ledgers found in box 129.

44. Local merchants in the July 2, 1927 *Rhinebeck Gazette* were said to be "in arms" over the delay in getting a good road run to Rhinebeck. As it was, construction on the "Hyde Park Road into Poughkeepsie" in 1926 took its toll on local business. A January 20, 1933 *Rhinebeck Gazette* article mentions a business meeting where attendees discussed writing on a sign just before Rhinebeck the projected date of opening "the new concrete highway." A 1934 U.S. Geological Survey map shows the improved road.

45. *The American Traveller* by D. Hewett, printed in 1825, is said to be the first travel guidebook on a national scope. It cites Rhinebeck one time on the route from New York City to Saratoga Springs (174). No town description is provided.

46. Both the Colles and the Princeton Cox maps (box 163, undated draft and an 1804 copy of 1803 map) seem to confirm this location by scaling. The Princeton map shows a large property called "Heirs of Jacob Tremper" with the next lot up labeled as "Asa Potter." It seems somewhat reasonable that Potter would take over a tavern, not build a new one right next door to an existing one, so that is the presumption for what happened to Trimper's. The "Ancient Documents" file at the Dutchess County Registry of Deeds contains a court document of Jacob Tremper dated May 4, 1767, in which he sued George Kramer of Rhinebeck, "tavernkeeper," for money owed him. Perhaps Tremper was leasing the building to Kramer as a tavern.

47. Dutchess County Surrogate Court archives, book A, page 132.

48. Buck, *Poughkeepsie Tax List Index*. Buck states that tax lists start in Dutchess County in 1717–18.

49. Two reasons exist for the broader use of Colles's map set. One, it had been more widely distributed through the years (now it is free on-line). The Erskine map collection is in the private collection of the New York Historical Society. The other reason is that the Colles collection is far easier to read.

50. Hasbrouck, *History of Dutchess County*, 45, 55.

51. Including a slight mix-up of the mills. He also appears to leave off houses depending on the map's intended use. The Starr Library has, arguably, the first version. It does not show East Market Street, but it shows Dr. Kiersted's house (not the later Heermance house). It also contains more data (possibly in draft form) than the next map. The next one is owned by the NYSA. This

richly colored and well-preserved map seems to be a cleaned-up version of the first. It labels the Kiersted home with the later name of Heermance (his son-in-law). Some argue this is the first map because it was the one submitted to the state, which still owns it. There is little doubt it was the one submitted, but we believe the Starr map was a slightly more detailed draft, done first. Hudson River Heritage (from the Janet Livingston/Montgomery Place collection) owns what appears to be the third version. This has a subsequent date on it of February 2, 1799. It looks like it was a copy of the first map (Kiersted home noted), but someone long ago tried, unsuccessfully, to draw in East Market Street. The Library of Congress now has the fourth version (obtained from a private collector in 2010), which is dated March 1800 and done for "Capt. Heermance" (noted on map). This one is colorful and detailed, but its condition makes it difficult to read some of the text. All but the Hudson River Heritage map are now accessible on the web.

52. American Scenic and Historic Preservation Society, *Twenty-Eighth Annual Report*, 121. Today it seems like an odd route (principally Route 28 across the river, up the Esopus Valley).

53. There is no obvious history behind this comment. The road "crosses" the Hudson and one option was it picked up the "Old Mine Road" which extended to, supposedly, ore mines. Perhaps there was a presumed connection to the Salisbury miners. The turnpike seems not to have officially followed the Old Mine Road on this side of the river; rather, it charted a more northern course toward Binghamton following the Onteora Trial (likely splitting near the present-day Route 209/28 intersection, near a notable bend in the Esopus Creek). Detailed mapmaker's notes for this western trek are in the NYSA (Cockburn Papers). The November 11, 1922 *Rhinebeck Gazette* has an article on the dedication of the stone monument.

54. The explosion of the violet industry in town can also be traced through these maps spanning thirty-seven years of change. Greenhouses begin showing up everywhere.

Chapter 3

55 Typical of newspaper ads and published schedules such as *Badger and Porter's Stage Register* (the bimonthly travel bible of the day in the northeast from 1825 to 1845), specific taverns are seldom mentioned, just the towns.

56. Holmes cites an advertisement in the *New-York Packet*, April 25, 1785 (which was unobtainable). The Mandeville Tavern seems to have turned into the Dusenbury Tavern. It later turned into the Holman House. The spy Major Andre was guarded here after his capture.

57. Weise, *History of Albany*, 389.

58. Vail, *Along the Hudson*, 489–96.

59. Ibid., 491. Control of the line on the east would require further research as Holmes (*Stagecoach East*) mentions Beach secured the west side and no mention of the east.

60. Morse, *Stage-Coach and Tavern Days*, quoting Longfellow, 371.

61. Hawthorne, *Note-Books of Nathanial Hawthorne*, 126–27.

62. Strickland, *Journal of a Tour*, 107–8.

63. An undated but likely circa 1798 large plot/map of Rhinebeck village in the Princeton Library, box 163, shows Asa Potter's name on property that appears to be across and just a few feet north of what is now Platt Avenue (this would seem to be a draft of the 1803 Cox map). Smith, *History of Rhinebeck*, 165, upon seeing the Starr copy of the Thompson map, also places Potter's Tavern near the Platt House (across from the Platt Avenue).

64. Stuart, James, *Three Years in North America*, 469.

65. Found at the American Antiquarian Society in Worcester, Massachusetts.

66. Early steamboats also had significant safety issues. Passengers would ride in barges pulled behind the steam tug just in case the boiler blew up. The technology was not improved until after the 1830s.

67. *St. Albans (VT) Daily Messenger*, May 21, 1902. They bought three at a cost of $17,000. There apparently were some delays getting the vehicles.

CHAPTER 4

68. The paper mill was right in town, where the Post Road crosses the Landsman Kill. It was the last mill to exist in the village area. Page 26 of the Rhinebeck Historical Society *Rhinebeck Album* notes a plaster mill near the "state road bridge." Sailing vessels used to bring gypsum rock down from Nova Scotia as ballast and the farmers used to cart it from Long Dock to this mill to be ground as fertilizer. The nine hydro sites are described in Smith, iv. He also cites sixteen mills (some on the same location).

69. DCRD, book 5, page 399. This is the 1746 triangle agreement. The actual 1719 deed is in the Princeton Library collection, Box 157. This

deed does not use this same wording; it makes no mention of mills. Another record also helps date this mill. In the "Special Session of the Road Commissioners, April 17, 1722 (from Supervisors Records of Dutchess County), p.50: "the straight and most Convenient way to the parting bounds of William Trophagen and Henry Beeckman and soe between theire bounds till over against the house of Said William Trophagen Ware a Road Stricks out westerly to the Landing of Kips Berrege and soepersueing the afore said high Road (Kings Highway) Southerly Leading along the <u>New Mill</u> of said Henry Beeckman..."

The lower mill, as discussed elsewhere, has a 1750 date attached to it, although an April 30, 1735 "Map for Richd Cookes" for six acres of land on the south side of the mill dam labels on the drawing "mills," so multiple mills were here before 1750. Box 157, Princeton Library. The storehouse shown on the 1769 map has a date of 1751, according to a journal entry in the Princeton Library Box 128, Folder 10.

70. Smith, *Province of New-York*, 197.

71. See supervisor of road record quote mentioned in chapter 5. Arie's brew house was somewhere between the Starr Library and the Rhinebeck Creek/present highway garage, but "a cornfield closer" to the library.

72. Ulster County Register of Deeds, book AA, page 377. The 1769 map seems to illustrate this property as being the northwestern most part of the tract (seemingly on Arie's side).

73. Smith, *Province of New-York*, 206. Smith mentions that the 1719 tract was on Crum Elbow Creek and mentioned in the deed to Jacobus Van Etten in 1721. Per the deed, "less some meadows," which seems some 60 acres, as Beekman records 230 acres sold in his account books (Princeton Archives).

74. See the genealogy page at http://home.earthlink.net/~petrakim/gdtree/61.html

75. Per Chris Brooks, Traphagen/Ostrander genealogist, up until after the English conquest of New Netherlands, people weren't required to have fixed surnames. While some families did, many times they also went by their patronymic rather than a surname. So Arie Hendricksen was the son of Hendrick Ariaensen because his father's first name was Hendrick. Hendrik's father's first name would have been Ariaen.

76. Ulster County Clerk, Archive Division, Board of Supervisors Minutes in Ulster County (pages 1, 4, 6 and 9). William shows up again in 1714, but neither name shows up by 1715, the next report available. Presumably, they were both busy with affairs in Dutchess County.

77. Hoes, *Baptismal and Marriage Registers*, 82.

78. Platt, *Second Book of Supervisors*, 18, 124.

79. Hasbrouck, *History of Dutchess County*, 45–50, and Smith, *History of Duchess County*, 60–61. All census, tax and Book of Supervisors data referenced comes from these county history sources.

80. Buck, *Poughkeepsie Tax List Index*. He provides: "William widow 1738/39—widow off Feb 1753–1774." "William 1741/42–June 1748" is also provided, but this must be William Jr.

81. This abbreviated genealogy is sourced from ancestry.com (except as noted) and confirmed by Chris Brooks. Since this book is about the BA and Post Road and not a genealogy study of the extended Traphagen family, research beyond this point is outside of the book's scope.

82. *Rhinebeck Gazette*, "The Traphagen Grist Mill on the Flatts," August 29, 1908. It reads: "From Aran Kee's collection we are permitted to take this interesting sketch. It is from the pen of an old resident who came to the flatts in 1828, and is long since dead. 'When William Traphagen made his purchase of land on "the flats" of Judge Beekman in 1706 a single mill site was included. This was west of the Post Road, on the north side of Landsman's Kill, at the foot of a ravine below mill hill. Forty-four years afterwards in 1750 his son William Traphagen, Jr., and his son-in-law Isaac Kool /Cole) built a mill that for nearly a century and a quarter was a land-mark of the locality. The date of its erection was marked on a beam 1750 W. T.-I. K. This was one of the customs of the times. The first miller was Isaac Kool or Cole as the name was afterwards written. After the revolution Col. Henry B. Livingston the owner of the upper mill bought the Traphagen mill and installed Daniel Mc Carty a soldier of the revolution as miller. Here Stephen and Robert Mc Carty as boys spent their early years. Later came James Hobbs as miller.'" The old resident writing mentions that it burned down on December 1, 1859, though 1869 is mentioned in a December 28, 1912 *RG* article titled "Looking Backwards" (*Rhinebeck Tribune* December 11, 1869: The old grist mill built in 1750 in the south western part of the village was burned to the ground Tuesday night. It was built by General Montgomery just prior to the Revolutionary War and was in active operation. The loss is $8,000). Thanks to Nancy Kelly for the 1908 article. This 1750 claim for a gristmill needs to be researched and verified, as does the location. If it is indeed the lower mill site, the 1769 map shows a single mill building here with two wheels. The 1779 map shows a single gristmill symbol. Two mills do appear on the 1798 map.

83. The original 1741 document is preserved in the NYSA in Albany. The actual 1736 will does not appear to exist. Arent's will is recorded in the DCRD, book 2, page 98.

84. Buck, *Rhinebeck Tax List Index*. He provides: "Arient Traphagen 1739/40 - widow 1746/47-June 1748."

85. A 1763 deed in the NYSA from his parents to his brother Johannes titles Simon as "Heir at Law" (at least through his branch of the family, but possibly across all the Traphagen siblings.)

CHAPTER 5

86. Spanning 1746–90, roughly forty-four total years of missing legal documents (wills, deeds, mortgages, licenses) and any other eighteenth-century records (journals, construction notes, bill of sales, early maps, newspaper articles) cloud history. The fact that not a scrap exists, after exhaustive searching, is surprising. Someone may have collected the material for an earlier book (pre-1880) and then lost it, or it could have been destroyed (there was a major fire in town in 1864).

87. The 1741 distribution and 1774 Bogardus/Kiersted agreement are held in the NYS Archives special collections; 1746 deed/plot is Book 5, page 399, DCRD, the original is in the new ancient docs book; 1769 map is in the Princeton University Library (Livingston Collection, Box 163); 1769 sale is Book 18, page 137 DCRD; 1770 survey and deed are in the Princeton University Library collection, Box 157; 1790 mortgage is Book 6, page 97 DCRD; 1802 sale is Book 17, page 534 (see also 18/599) DCRD. Arent Traphagen's will also exists in the DCRD, Book 2, page 97, but it only serves to distribute his property equally amongst his children. Note that the 1769 map contains a sketchy date reference of November 24, 1769, in the torn bottom left legend. It may not be indicative of when the map was created. Given that it refers to a property "to be conveyed," which was properly conveyed in 1770, and the "Coll" is deceased (this is Judge Henry, the original patentee, who died in 1716, not Colonel Henry, who died in 1776), 1769 could be the date created.

88. Princeton University Collection, box 128, folder 10. See list of plots of Colonel Beekman upon his death.

89. Though we were extremely diligent creating our maps using exact angles, declinations and distances, we, the authors, did not do so with the help of sophisticated mapping software and recognize we could

have introduced our own small errors. (We used a number of tools including the free program Tractplotter.com.) The scale of the online Parcel Access map we used could also have been imprecise, introducing more errors. There were also errors in the old deeds, maps and plots. Therefore, the map presented here is not definitive; it is our best estimate of the lot layouts based on the analysis of the data available. A few other configurations were considered, but they all had significant, unexplainable issues. Due to these issues, showing more granularity than what we show would erroneously imply exactness that the data does not support. It would also make the map confusing.

90. Arent's property begins at the southwestern most corner of the mill lot, extends north 895 feet, then follows the 21 degree border, and then it seems to extend into Geesje's home lot. If this occurs, Geesje's property would not be the twenty-two acres specified; rather, it would measure fourteen acres. Geesje's property abuts the 1705 boundary line to the west, so it cannot possibly be pushed back. The 1774 agreement between Bogardus and Kiersted seems to give Kiersted clear title to whatever Arent property was within the Geesje home lot area (so it seems his lot did extend into Geesje's). This agreement gives Kiersted the whole area of Geesje's home lot, as well as the area just north of it (to the west of the back of the Oak Street lots).

91. The Beekman copy is also notable because the house sketch is drawn slightly inside the triangle. It is likely just that: a rough sketch. Box 157, Princeton Library.

92. Platt, *Book of the Supervisors*, 51.

93. Notably, in 1810, it was on Livingston land, but how long the Livingstons had it would need to be researched.

94. Morse, *Historic Old Rhinebeck*, 246. From the sketch provided by Morse, the building appears to have added a second story by his time. He claims this old stone house looked much like the Abraham Kip House down on 6 Long Dock Road. Born in 1842, Morse surely saw this old building before it was demolished.

95. DCRD, book 27, page 111.

96. This is an interesting piece of land. Kiersted seems to have gotten it with the Cole property he bought in 1769. Then Simon had it surveyed on March 27, 1770, and he bought back from Kiersted on July 3, 1770 (both docs in Princeton Library, box 157). It shows up in the February 12, 1790 Bogardus mortgage (book 6, page 97), being excluded and described as "one acre of Simon I Cole on the north side of road," then again in 1802 release of the

Bogardus estate to Benjamin (book 18, page 599) "exclusive of one acre where the store stands." It is later described in the 1802 sale to Asa Potter (book 17, page 534), as the seller excluded "one acre...occupied by store of Martin Heermance." The use as a store (or unoccupied building) would give some explanation why Randel (1810) failed to mark this structure on his map. The Thompson maps highlight one or two houses between the corner and Kiersted's, depending on the version.

97. By 1763, Geesje's home lot was in the hand of Johannes Cool, their son (and Simon's younger brother), through a deed archived in the NYSA, so Hans Kiersted likely could not buy it sooner. What happened to Geesje and Isaac is unknown. They may have moved closer to the mill they seemed to have co-owned.

98. DCRD, book 1, page 380, January 1, 1719. We did not conduct deed research on lots south of the Landsman Kill.

99. Morse, *Historic Old Rhinebeck*, 91. Morse describes a property on Montgomery Street north of the BA bounded on the west by Arent's property, so it is possible Arent owned the area covering Oak Street.

100. The original six acres were described as "a certain parcel of ground... Laying on ye north side of Landsman Kill Beginning at his [Traphagen's] Southeastern most angle by a white pine tree marked standing on ye top of a Faale of water in said Kill Thence to Run a Long his bounds from said tree so far that a Stright Shall Intersectt moving a Stright Line to Intersect ye Line Drawn to said Tree so that it may Comprehend Six acres of Land." Princeton Library, box 157. William's signature and stamp are affixed to the deed.

101. Simon also had a son named Simon (and a son Peter), as well as a grandson named Simon (and Jacob). Given the dates, it is likely Geesje's son Simon is named on this map. There is also a chance—given how grossly this map was drawn—that the structure shown was Arent's house located at the upper triangle corner. We believe it is not.

102. It is even possible the next owner of this property, Everardus Bogardus, had something to do with the building being constructed. He had wealth and a vision for business.

103. September 8, 1753 survey done for Henry Beekman. Princeton Library, box 157. It includes a map symbol of the church, as well as the mills and shows the Post Road. Given it was a survey of the east side of the road, anything on the west side may just not have been included, so one cannot read too much into this.

104. This hypothesis was suggested by Chris Brooks. The tax list is Buck's.

105. Dutchess County Probate/Surrogate Court records (County courthouse), Book A, p.25. Witnessed September 22, 1787. Simon's other son, Peter, is mentioned briefly. It does not say deceased, but everything he should get skips over him to his children. Simon also had three daughters: Margaret, wife of Herman Snyder; Margery, wife of James Scott (deceased); and Beleitie, wife of "Leg."

CHAPTER 6

106. The March 27, 1770 Cole survey mentioned previously labels the boundary property as "Traphagen Home Lot" (and the July 3, 1770 indenture refers to it as "Arent's Home Lot") and notably, not that of Bogardus. It is hard to really tell what this implies, but it may show the BA property had not been sold to Bogardus yet.

107. Buck, *Rhinebeck Tax List Index*.

108. The October 6, 1774 deed is in the NYSA manuscript collection. Bogardus gives Kiersted clear title to land in exchange for "the like release of his respective House Lot and wood Land agreeable to this division & the further consideration of six pence to him paid." This deed describes property being given to Kiersted that was seemingly on Arent's home lot. The deed does not include the BA triangle lot. It is unlikely, but remotely possible, that Bogardus and Traphagen were somehow even related. Often interfamily estate transfers were not fully recorded.

109. Bogardus, *Dear "Cousin,"* chart 1, 9, 9A.

110. Besides the deeds mentioned, there are at least four others listing him as merchant (in the NYSA, Livingston Collection, box 2, folder 2, January 1, 1787; May 31, 1787; and June 1, 1787 [for land near where the Landsman Kill and Rhinebeck Kill join]), from Colonel Henry Livingston, Gentlemen, to Everardus Bogardus, Merchant. There is also a deed dated September 18, 1789, in the NYSA between Bogardus and Kiersted and again with the merchant designation.

111. Hasbrouck, *History of Dutchess County*, 109. This source contains the list of who signed and who did not. Helen Delaporte, former head of the local DAR, wrote after some investigation: "The land proprietors were all patriots, while the rank and file of the tenants were indifferent. Some were outspoken loyalists, and many refused to sign until they had weighed the matter. Large numbers of these are enrolled in the later regiments." Her comments were printed in an undated *Rhinebeck Gazette* article under

the title of "Revolutionary Records of Northern Dutchess," which were reprinted in the Rhinebeck Historical Society, *Rhinebeck Album*, 9.

112. General Montgomery's life and dedication to the patriotic cause (he was an Irishman), is the subject of many books. Room in this book on the Beekman Arms is limited, so we cannot give him more than a sentence. His life was epic and anyone reading this footnote should go about learning more of him.

113. Rhinebeck Historical Society, *A Rhinebeck Album*, 28. See notes of William Smith, a Whig imprisoned in the Livingston house. Smith's assertions could not be validated.

114. Kelly, *Brief History of Rhinebeck*, 27.

115. Morse, *Historic Old Rhinebeck*, 229. Morse places an Everardus Bogardus as a lieutenant in the "5th company" raised in Rhinebeck, but nothing exists to support this assertion—plus, he was home receiving letters from his brother. As a businessman and producer of goods, his role in the community was likely still valuable to the army and its logistical supply chain. There was another Everardus (son of Everardus), cousin to Rhinebeck's Everardus. He likely was living in Kingston.

116. This can be found searching Fultonhistory.org or in the pamphlet *A Rhinebeck Album*.

117. DCRD, book 18, page 599.

118. DCRD Ancient Documents Book (index) and originals tracked down by the county historian.

119. Another hypothesis is this property reverted briefly back to Janet Montgomery due to Everardus's financial ills (it would seem to still be under the Traphagen "6 schilling forever" lease). Nothing in the historic records speaks to this possibility.

Chapter 7

120. We had this fact confirmed by a Washington scholar at the University of Virginia. There is also no evidence George Washington ever visited Henry Beekman Livingston in the Beekman House in Rhinecliff. That, too, was local lore. The state historic site at Clermont has a letter dated June 1782 from Margaret Beekman to her son Chancellor Robert Livingston mentioning that Martha Washington stayed at her house.

121. The legend further continues that Margaret and Thomas were married on February 22, 1779, at a ceremony in the RDC that used English for the very first

time. Adding to the story, a set of tables supposedly given to the Tillotsons by George Washington was in the possession of Olin Dows. He willed them to the state historic site at Clermont when he passed away (they are undocumented). Washington was in lower New York during this time, as Stony Point (the battle was fought there in July) and the defense of the Hudson were on his mind.

122. Schoonmaker, *History of Kingston*, 335–39.

123. *Kingston (NY) Rising Sun*, April 26, 1794, in the archives of the AAS.

124. In fact, the few letters with a Rhinebeck reference in existence are complimentary letters to Janet Livingston, sister of Gertrude Livingston, Morgan Lewis's wife. These were dated 1778. Burr had served under Janet's husband, Richard Montgomery, in Quebec. Burr's paper collection is extensive. While a rudimentary search found nothing, research would need to be done to definitively state that the Morse comments are not fully accurate. A review of the Morgan Lewis papers in the New York Historical Society did not find any mention of a contested Rhinebeck campaign. A note on party affiliations: there is a complicated evolution of the Democratic and Republican parties, both deriving from the Democratic-Republicans. This party opposed the Federalists, a party that no longer exists. Burr and Lewis both seemed to be members of the Democratic-Republicans, but this was probably at a time when the party was splitting and factioning into different alliances.

125. This gets complicated, but there was a speech given by Hamilton in the Albany home of Judge John Taylor that seemed to agitate Burr. The son of a local Rhinebeck doctor named Cooper attended this house party and wrote a letter to Philip Schuyler, Hamilton's father-in-law and father to Philip Schuyler Jr. of Rhinebeck. The letter somehow got published in the Albany paper, and Burr demanded an apology for its content.

126. This ad shows up in a number of places. In Alice Morse Earle's *Stagecoach and Tavern Days*, 1900, it is found on page 276. It is also in a 1905 article titled "Along the Hudson in Stage-Coach Days," by Vail. Both were published before Morse's work, so he may have seen them. Whether or not the ad itself is really authentic remains questionable.

CHAPTER 8

127. Hasbrouck, *History of Dutchess County*, 55. Federal Census of 1790.

128. Benjamin's brother Nicholas (with the designation "lately" next to his name) also appears on this 1802 reacquisition of the property deed, book

18, page 599, DCRD. However, Nicholas appears to have passed away in 1794 (so "lately" probably means he passed away but was officially on record). Unexplainably, the previous 1790 mortgage Everardus had out to George and William Ludlow was not recorded as officially discarded until August 29, 1804.

129. See obituary in the November 2, 1802 *Providence (RI) Gazette* (held in the AAS). See complaint by Asa Potter against M. Livingston, who seems to have tried to defame his character. Found in the DCRD Ancient Documents book, dated October 10, 1788.

130. Asa's will is in the records of the Surrogate Court in Poughkeepsie, Book B, Page 547. It is signed October 9, 1805. William Jaques is listed as a witness.

131. Some of the first significant changes in land ownership law were the outcome of New York's anti-rent movement. In 1839, a series of riots and altercations between tenants, landlords and the police began that eventually spread across eleven counties. It became a big part of the politics of the day. The New York constitutional convention of 1846 even featured an allodial title amendment that replaced the arbitrary feudal rent system with a guarantee of absolute property ownership. It failed, but court decisions in the 1850s began to limit the worst features of the manorial system.

132. Per table in Welles, *Reminiscences*. This is the only place it is mentioned. Morse says William retired.

133. Repeated in the *Pine Plains (NY) Register Herald*, August 17, 1983. May have come from Morse, *Historic Old Rhinebeck*, 327.

134. He is buried toward the far back corner of the RDC cemetery, and notably, his name is spelled "Jaques." A second William Jaques's grave is in the Rhinebeck Cemetery with a date of passing, strangely, one month after the first William. It is thought that since the RDC cemetery was closed for burial shortly after William, the second grave is for his wife Mary (aka Polly), and they simply inscribed William's name on it. It is not known if William was actually moved here. William's son Benjamin (died 1837, age twenty-one) is buried next to him in the RDC. Benjamin's passing may be why the Jaqueses left the BA.

135. Jacob Trimper died around 1789, and his sons were Harmanus, John, Jacob, Jon Jacob and George. See April 6, 1918 *Rhinebeck Gazette* article for the steamboat reference.

136. Tiertjen, *Portrait of a Town*, 49. The author notes that the plant was on Garden Street extension, and oil gas was obtained by spraying oil over

a bed of hot coal or coke. Only six customers were left in 1901 when electricity came.

CHAPTER 9

137. The *Rhinebeck Gazette* on Tuesday April 19, 1864, (though difficult to read the date) notes "James McElroy, the popular host of the Rhinebeck Hotel, has sold the Hotel property to McIntyre & Hoffman for $9,000." It is not clear who McIntyre was, as he/she was not on the deed (Book 127, p. 399).

138. See the *Pine Plains Register*, "The Beekman Arms: A Link with Bygone Years," Summer 1974.

139. Kelly, *Brief History of Rhinebeck*, 45. The *Rhinebeck Gazette* reference is found here. It is assumed the year is meant to be 1865.

140. Philip, *Rhinecliff*, 66–67.

141. Unpublished genealogical study of the Tremper family by Priscilla Tremper Leith, 17. A copy is owned by the RHS.

142. For George, see the March 31, 1890 *Poughkeepsie Daily Eagle*; For Alvin, see the March 18, 1881 *Red Hook Journal*. Alvin passed away at the "Hudson River Insane Asylum" after a lingering illness.

143. The May 2, 1891 *Rhinebeck Gazette* notes: "Mr. Lasher, the new lessee of the Rhinebeck Hotel, took possession yesterday," so he was more than a manager; he actually leased it. Strangely, the *Red Hook Journal* of September 8, 1893, notes, "Nicholas Hoffman, proprietor of the Rhinebeck Hotel, will enlarge that hostelry." Page 6 of the *Poughkeepsie Daily Eagle* on January 26, 1894, mentions the Rhinebeck Hotel was sold on Tuesday by the owner, Nicholas Hoffman, to Vernon D. Lake. Fulmer is the only name on the deed to Lake. Her connection to Nicholas and Robert is not known, but she was likely their sister.

144. A rare copy is owned by the New York Historical Society. The society's copy is actually an "updated" copy reproduced by W.W. Foster around 1914. He changed the cover and removed the photos but kept the original writing intact and added five pages. LaForge and the Winne estate have the two known copies of the original, but others are probably buried in attics all over.

145. A November 16, 1907 *Rhinebeck Gazette* article mentions that Halleck Welles and two others were being cross-examined in a Grand Jury investigation into a forgery case. Details were not provided so it is not

clear what side he was on. A January 17, 1928 *Rhinebeck Gazette* article mentions his departure to Long Island.

CHAPTER 11

146. Lathrop, *Early American Inns and Taverns*, 263.
147. Dows kept a diary, but the years 1912–26 are missing. According to David Byars, a current biographer, the 1927–29 entries do not say anything specific about the BA. Harrie Lindeberg had several architectural books and articles published (by him and others), but none mentions the BA. It is almost as if the hotel design was a throw-in, a favor done by Lindeberg after having been commissioned to design a dozen or so buildings at Fox Hollow. Daughter Deborah's 1986 recorded reminiscences of her life mention the BA a few times, though nothing comes from the initial period (she was young and likely not involved with her father's specific business).
148. *Rhinebeck Gazette*, "Open House at Beekman Arms," September 15, 1917. On April 15, 1927, the *Poughkeepsie Eagle* in its "10 Years Ago'" column mentioned the jacket story.
149. He appreciated the hotel's past and added to Halleck Welles's collection of antiques. The large barometer behind the front desk was his. In the taproom hangs a picture of the steam yacht *Mohican* that he once owned before 1905.
150. See 1986 Dow tapes held in the RHS.
151. *Rhinebeck Gazette*, December 19, 1903. This included horses, harnesses, feed and wagons. The original barn on this site appears sometime between 1886 and 1895, according to the Sanborn maps. The cause of the fire was arson. It was set by the owner of two of the horses to collect on the insurance. He got eight years in Sing-Sing.
152. "An American Manor House: 'Fox Hollow Farm' The Country Place of Tracy Dows, Esq.," *Architectural Record*, 311.
153. According to his obituary in the February 22, 1962 *Rhinebeck Gazette*, Foster operated the hotel until 1925. The ousting of Foster may or may not have been as dramatic as court documents suggest; it is difficult to tell. Foster's divorce in 1922 may have factored in, and he had no control over the economy. He seems to have advertised enough and done his best to try to get the business going. Foster was back in town by 1933, opening Foster's Coach House a few doors north on Montgomery Street (which he held until 1954).
154. Material on Lewis Winne was found in an article/interview entitled "Was Your Business Normal in 1931?" published in the *Business Pulse-O-*

Meter. No future identification is provided. This article was found in the extensive scrapbook collection held by Lewis Winne's descendants still living locally. Lewis amassed a sizable personal collection of clippings, photos and other ephemera covering his long tenure.

CHAPTER 12

155. An August 17, 1939 *Rhinebeck Gazette* article mentions this syndicate included fourteen men. In addition to Lewis Winne, Pierre Cookingham, Olin Dows, Benson Frost and Dr. Buckeley, there also was Henry Billings, Alvah Frost, Ralph Pitcher, Clarence Rhynders, Henry Schaad, Jacob Strong, Oakleigh Cookingham, Dr. Merrick Phillips and Stanton R. Tremper. None of these names seems to appear on any legal documents found. The names of those in this eight-person consortium are based on county records and local knowledge.

156. Olin Dows is also locally famous for painting the murals in the Rhinebeck and Hyde Park Post Offices. Also, technically only Bulkeley, Cookingham and Frost are on the first deed. They sold to the new Beekman Arms Inc., held by all these men, on January 15, 1940.

157. See correspondence on the Rhinebeck post office in the Franklin D. Roosevelt Presidential Library.

158. Franklin D. Roosevelt, "Address at the Dedication of the New Post Office in Rhinebeck, New York," May 1, 1939, Franklin D. Roosevelt Presidential Library (also on-line.)

CHAPTER 13

159. Taken from an unlabeled culinary magazine article from the 1970s but confirmed in person with Mr. LaForge.

160. Henry Delamater, founder of the First National Bank of Rhinebeck, had his house built in 1844 by Alexander Jackson Davis, who was perhaps the most famous architect of "Domestic Gothic" of his time.

161. Another archaeological dig is mentioned in a July 17, 1954 edition of the *Utica Daily Press*. It mentions a dig was done twenty years earlier while excavating the basement. A branding iron with the initials EB (suggested to be Everardus Bogardus) was found along with some other small objects. All of these objects were on display but were stolen during the LaForge era.

162. An amusing 1970s-era anecdote comes from Chuck LaForge. So typical of the '70s, PVC plastic tubing cannons were fitted on the front lawn as decorations. This was done much to the delight of those customers who were slightly inebriated, as they often took pleasure moving these about.

163. When opened, it is claimed that *Esquire* magazine called it one of its "Best New Restaurants" and the *New York Times* put it on its list of "10 Best Destination Restaurants." This is mentioned in various Larry Forgione bios on the Internet, including at starchef.com.

CHAPTER 14

164. The deed is only a token $10, with the total consideration paid in not publically disclosed (the tax value is $4.5m). The Delamater House transacted separately. Regarding most of the valuable guns and artifacts still on display, LaForge felt they belonged to the hotel, so he naturally passed them onto the next owner. The Bantas have also been active in collecting historical material on the inn and display what they have found. None of the documents currently hanging have anything directly to do with the origins of the hotel.

CHAPTER 16

165. Only a copy of the map still exists according to the Dutchess County Historian. Therefore, it cannot be confirmed if the word "Hotel" is original to this map. The timing of ownership does seem to offer support that it is from 1802, as does the note we put in the caption for this map.

166. All of this data is current website information as of December 2013.

CHAPTER 17

167 The actual location of this inn is a little difficult to pin down, as the roads in this area moved around a bit. Town historian Nancy Kelly said, "It is on the north side of Patten road as you enter from Route 308 across from 781 Route 308. There is myrtle still growing there, and the site was always pointed out to me."

168. Morse, *Historic Old Rhinebeck*, 245. Morse mentions there were two old taverns here: "The Bowery had two, the residence of the late Stephen and James C.

McCarty being one before they owned it, and the Brinckerhoff-Pultz, later called the Bowery house, the other." The first one has no other history.

169. Ruge's is at 6444 Montgomery Street at the corner of Chestnut. This assumes Tammany was Kip's. Elise Lathrop in her book *Early American Inns and Taverns* (264) calls the Bowery on East Market Street "Tammany Hall." She is almost certainly mistaken.

170. A large eight-box collection of Lewis papers is held at the New York Historical Society. An examination of these documents did not find any support for the Rhinebeck political battle. Any Morgan Lewis's papers in Ogden Mills historic site have never been accessioned and are inaccessible, according to administrators.

171. At first, Morse says it is across from Livingston Street. Later, on page 281, he strangely now claims he made a mistake earlier in the book and that instead of saying it was opposite Livingston Street, he should have said Chestnut Street.

172. Or the final version published in 1803 ("copied in 1804"). These maps had been held locally at Montgomery Place (a few miles north in Annandale-on-Hudson) but are now in Princeton. The Delafield Family Papers and the Edward Livingston Papers held there were given to the University Library in 1986 by Mr. J. Dennis Delafield (class of 1957) and Professor Penelope D. Johnston. These maps are in Box 163. The lots of Asa Potter (who had an inn) and Jacob Tremper (who had an inn much earlier) are right next to each other. Using the crude map scales, Potter's seemed to be 1,617 feet from the Market Street corner, and Trimper's was 1,568 feet, but there is far too much imprecision in these measurements to tell much. The taverns could have been one and the same building.

Bibliography

BOOKS

Aitken, William B. *Distinguished Families in America Descended from Wilhelmus Beekman and Jan Thomasse Van Dyke*. New York: Knickerbocker Press, 1912.

Bayles, W. Harrison. *Old Taverns of New York*. New York: Frank Allaben Genealogical Company, 1915.

Blanchard, Frank. *History of the Reformed Dutch Church of Rhinebeck Flatts*. Albany, NY: J.B. Lyon Company, 1931.

Bogardus, William B. *Dear "Cousin": A Charted Genealogy of the Descendants of Anneke Jans Bogardus (1605–1663) to the 5th Generation*. Wilmington, OH: self-published through Penobscot Press, 1996.

Buck, Clifford, M., comp. *Poughkeepsie, Rhinebeck, Northeast Tax List Index*. Salt Point, NY: unpublished (copy in the Adriance Library), undated.

Colles, Christopher. *A Survey of the Roads of the United States of America*. New York: self-published, 1789.

Comstock, Sarah. *Old Road from the Heart of New York*. New York: Knickerbocker Press, 1915.

Drury, Reverend John B. *The Reformed (Dutch) Church of Rhinebeck: An Historical Address Delivered at the 150th Anniversary of its Organization*. Chatham, NY: Courier Steam Printing House, 1881.

Dutchess County Historical Society. *Yearbook of the Dutchess County Historical Society, 1918* (Includes a brief history of Thomas Inn). Poughkeepsie, NY: Dutchess County Historical Society, 1918.

Dunbar, Seymour. *A History of Travel in America*. Vols. 1 and 2. Indianapolis, IN: Bobbs-Merrill Company, 1915.

Earle, Alice Morse. *Stage-Coach and Tavern Days*. New York: The MacMillan Company, 1911.

Eberlin, Harold D., and Cortlandt Van Dyke Hubbard. *Historic Houses of the Hudson Valley*. New York: Bonanza Books, 1942.

Frazier, Michael. *Images of America: Rhinebeck*. Charleston, SC: Arcadia Publishing, 1912.

Hasbrouck, Frank, ed. *The History of Dutchess County, New York*. Poughkeepsie, NY: S.A. Matthieu, 1909.

Hawthorne, Nathanial. *Passages from the American Note-Books of Nathanial Hawthorne*. Boston: Houghton, Mifflin and Company, 1885.

———. *The Snow-Image and Other Twice-told Tales*. Boston: Ticknor, Reed, and Fields, 1853.

Hendricks, Howard. *The City of Kingston, Birth Place of New York State*. Kingston, NY: Kingston Board of Trade. 1902.

Hine, C.G. *The New York and Albany Post Road*. New York: C.G. Hine, 1905.

———. *The Old Mine Road*. Kingston, NY: Hines Annual, 1908.

Historical and Genealogical Record, Dutchess and Putnam Counties, New York. Poughkeepsie, NY: A.V. Haight Co., 1912.

Hoes, Roswell R. *Baptismal and Marriage Registers of the Old Dutch Church of Kingston*. New York: De Vinne Press, 1891.

Holmes, Oliver W., and Peter T. Rohrbach. *Stagecoach East*. Washington, DC: Smithsonian Institution Press, 1983.

Hudson, William L. *Rambles in Colonial Byways*. Vol. 1. Philadelphia: J.B. Lippincott Company, 1906.

Jenkins, Stephen. *The Greatest Street in the World*. New York: Knickerbocker Press, 1911.

Lathrop, Elise. *Early American Inns and Taverns*. New York: Tutor Publishing Company, 1926.

Lindeberg, Harrie T. *Domestic Architecture of Harrie T. Lindeberg*. New York: Acanthus Press, 2003.

Lossing, Benson J. *The Hudson from the Wilderness to the Sea*. New York: Virtue & Yorston, 1866.

Kelly, Frank B., comp. *Historical Guide to the City of New York* (includes Nash, George W., *Post Roads and Milestones*, 371–76). New York: Frederick A. Stokes, 1909.

Kelly, Nancy V. *A Brief History of Rhinebeck: The Living Past of a Hudson Valley Community*. New York: Wise Family Trust, 2001.

———. *Rhinebeck's Historic Architecture*. Charleston, SC: The History Press, 2009.

Morse, Howard H. *Historic Old Rhinebeck Echoes of Two Centuries*. Rhinebeck, NY: self-published, 1908.

Munsell, Joel. *Annals of Albany*. Vol. 1. Albany, NY: J. Munsell, 1850.

Palmer, Richard, F. *The "Old Line Mail": Stagecoach Days in Upstate New York*. Utica, NY: North Country Books, 1977.

Pelletreau, William S. *History of Putnam County, New York*. Philadelphia: W.W. Preston & Co., 1886.

Philip, Cynthia Owen. *Rhinecliff, The Tangled Tale of Rhinebeck's Waterfront: A Hudson River History*. Hensonville, NY: Black Dome Press, 2008.

Platt, Edmund. *Book of the Supervisors of Dutchess County N.Y. AD.1718–1722*. Poughkeepsie, NY: Vassar Brothers Institute, 1908.

———. *The Eagle's History of Poughkeepsie*. Poughkeepsie, NY: Platt and Platt, 1905.

———. *Old Miscellaneous Records of Dutchess County, The Second Book of Supervisors and Assessors*. Poughkeepsie, NY: Vassar Brothers Institute, 1909.

Relief Hook and Ladder Company. *Illustrated Rhinebeck*. Rhinebeck, NY: Rhinebeck Gazette, 1896.

Rhinebeck Historical Society. *A Rhinebeck Album, 1776, 1876, 1976*. Rhinebeck, NY: Rhinebeck Historical Society, 1976.

Rice, Kym S. *Early American Taverns: For the Entertainment of Friends and Strangers*. Chicago: Regnery Gateway, 1983.

Scharf, John T. *History of Westchester County*. Bronx, NY: L.E. Preston & Company, 1886.

Schoonmaker, Marius. *The History of Kingston, New York*. New York: Burr Printing House, 1888.

Smith, Edward M. *Documentary History of Rhinebeck*. Rhinebeck, NY: self-published, 1881.

Smith, James H. *History of Duchess County*. Syracuse, NY: D. Mason & Co., 1882.

Smith, Philip H. *General History of Duchess County, from 1609 to 1876, Inclusive*. Pawling, NY: self-published, 1877.

Smith, William. *The History of the Late Province of New-York*. London: Thomas Wilcox, 1756.

State of New York. *Colonial Laws of New York From the Year 1664 to the Revolution*. Vols. 1–5. Albany, NY: James B. Lyon, State Printer, 1894.

————. *Laws of State of New York Passed at 119ᵗʰ Session of the Legislature.* Vol. 1. Albany, NY: James B. Lyon, Printer, 1896.

————. *Laws of the State of New York, Comprising the Constitution, and the Acts of the Legislature, since the Revolution, from the First to the Twentieth Session, Inclusive.* Vol. 3. New York: Thomas Greenleaf, November 1797.

Strickland, William. *Journal of a Tour in the United States of America, 1794–1795.* New York: New York Historical Society, 1971.

Stuart, James. *Three Years in North America.* Volume 1. Edinburgh: Robert Cadell, 1833.

Verplank, William E., and Moses W. Collyer. *The Sloops of the Hudson.* New York: Knickerbocker Press, 1908.

Weise, Arthur J. *The History of the City of Albany, New York.* Albany: E.H. Binder, 1884.

Welles, Halleck. *Reminiscences of the Oldest Hotel in America 1700–1907.* Rhinebeck, NY: self-published, 1907.

Magazine Articles/Reports

American Scenic and Historic Preservation Society, Twenty-Eighth Annual Report, 1922–23 (to the State Legislature). New York: J.B. Lyons Co., 1923.

"An American Manor House: 'Fox Hollow Farm' The Country Place of Tracy Dows, Esq." *The Architectural Record* 30 (July–December 1911): 311–26.

Floyd-Jones, Elbert. *A Relic of the Highway: The Origin and Use of Mile-Stones,* Appendix B of the Twenty-Eighth Annual Report of the American Scenic and Historic Preservation Society, 1922–23. New York: J.B. Lyons Co., 1923.

Gehring, Charles T., and William A. Starna. "Dutch and Indians in the Hudson Valley: The Early Period." *The Hudson Valley Regional Review* 9, no. 2 (September 1992): 1–25.

Kelly, Nancy V. "Rhinebeck: Transition in 1799." *The Hudson Valley Regional Review* 6, no. 2 (March 1989): 70–99.

McDermott, William P. "Colonial Land Grants in Dutchess County, NY. A Case Study in Settlement." *The Hudson Valley Regional Review* 3, no. 2 (September 1986): 1–19.

Saylor, Henry H. "The Best Twelve Country Houses in America: Foxhollow Farm at Rhinebeck, NY." *Country Life in America* 29 (1915–16): 25–28.

Spratt, James. "Milestones of Dutchess County." *The Hudson River Valley Review* 26, no. 2 (Spring 2010): 109–114.

Stevens, John A. "Old New York Taverns." *Harper's New Monthly Magazine* 80 (April 1890): 842.

Vail, R.P.H. "Along the Hudson in Stage-Coach Days." *The Outlook* 80 (1905): 489–96.

NEWSPAPERS CITED

Armenia (NY) Harlem Valley Times, May 24, 1913

Elmira (NY) Morning Telegram, July 14, 1907

Greenleaf's New York Journal, January 22, 1794

Kingston (NY) Rising Sun, April 26, 1794

New York City Chronicle Express, April 12, 1804

New York City Republican Watch-Tower, May 28, 1800

New York City Spirit of the Times, September 26, 1874

New York Daily Tribune, July 19, 1851

New York Mercantile Advertiser, May 22, 1802

New York Times, November 2, 1936; November 8, 1932

Pine Plains (NY) Register, Summer 1974

Pine Plains (NY) Register Herald, August 17, 1983

Poughkeepsie (NY) Daily Eagle, April 11, 1894; January 26, 1894; March 31, 1890;

Poughkeepsie (NY) Eagle, April 15, 1927

Poughkeepsie (NY) Eagle-News, July 1, 1931; November 5, 1940

Poughkeepsie (NY) Star Enterprise, November 3, 1937

Providence (RI) Gazette, November 2, 1802

Putnam County (NY) Republican, August 22, 1940

Red Hook (NY) Journal, March 18, 1881; September 8, 1893

Rhinebeck (NY) Gazette, various editions as noted throughout

St. Albans (VT) Daily Messenger, May 21, 1902

Utica (NY) Daily Press, July 17, 1954

Index

About the Authors

MATTHEW PLUMB is a history and English major at the University of Massachusetts and hopes to continue writing and making history more accessible and meaningful to readers. He also studies Irish traditional music on the guitar and fiddle. He is studying abroad in Oxford on scholarship during the summer of 2014.

BRIAN PLUMB, a native of Hyde Park, New York, grew up fascinated by those small milestones along the Post Road. He also witnessed the bicentennial events on the lawn of the Beekman Arms long ago. Both left impressions that sparked his lifelong interest in Hudson Valley history. He has previously written *A History of Longfellow's Wayside Inn* (The History Press, 2011) and is a member of that inn's colonial music ensemble. Professionally he serves as director of finance for a large energy company and holds an MBA and a BSME. He and his family live in the Boston area with their half-pug, Ed. The authors can be reached at: TheBeekmanArms@ gmail.com.